PUTNAM'S REVOLUTIONARY WAR WINTER ENCAMPMENT

THE HISTORY AND ARCHAEOLOGY OF PUTNAM MEMORIAL STATE PARK

DANIEL CRUSON

THE History PRESS

Israel Putnam, the commander of the Redding winter camps.

To Kathleen von Jena, who should have been the coauthor of this book.

Published by The History Press
Charleston, SC 29403
www.historypress.net

First published 2011

Manufactured in the United States

ISBN 978.1.60949.231.1

Cruson, Daniel.
Putnam's Revolutionary War winter encampment : the history and archaeology of Putnam Memorial State Park / Daniel Cruson.
p. cm.
Includes bibliographical references and index.
ISBN 978-1-60949-231-1
1. Putnam Memorial State Park (Conn.)--History. 2. Putnam Memorial State Park (Conn.)--Antiquities. 3. Connecticut--History--Revolution, 1775-1783. 4. Fairfield County (Conn.)--History--Revolution, 1775-1783. I. Title.
F102.F2C78 2011
974.6'03--dc23
2011041043

Notice: The information in this book is true and complete to the best of our knowledge. It is offered without guarantee on the part of the author or The History Press. The author and The History Press disclaim all liability in connection with the use of this book.

Contents

Preface

When I was in elementary school, my grandfather took me to the yearly church picnics, which were always held at Putnam Park. Here, besides learning how to drink root beer like a man, I spent many pleasant hours climbing among the collapsed chimney remains, peeping into Philip's Cave and standing in awe in front of the cases of Revolutionary War firearms in the little museum. Here, not twelve inches in front of my face, were some of the actual weapons that were used against the British to secure our independence. Several times, as I walked back over to the Company Street, where the remains of the enlisted men's huts lay in two meandering rows, I felt the overwhelming desire to dig among the rocks to see if I could find things that were dropped or lost by the soldiers. It took me forty years, but in 1998, I finally got my wish.

The park suffered from neglect in the period of the 1960s through the early 1990s. There had been some archaeology done there by David Poirier in the mid-1970s, but his funding ran out, and little was done with his findings beyond a couple of modest journal articles. Another archaeological assessment was conducted by Ricardo Elias from the University of Boston in 1991. Its purpose was to inventory all of the visible features and conduct some subsurface testing to evaluate the nature and extent of the military site. Later in that same year, state history enthusiasts were given a rude slap in the face when then governor Lowell Wiecker closed the park and pulled out all of its staff in what was claimed to be a budget shortfall.

The park remained closed for the next six years. The only reason that the park property did not fall into complete ruin was because of the neighbors, who insisted on cutting the lawns and trimming some brush, all on their own time and without compensation. This group of concerned neighbors formed the nucleus of a nonprofit corporation called the Friends and Neighbors of Putnam Park (FANS), an organization that has continued to the present, with members volunteering their time to create programs for the public and continuing to serve as advocates for the park's maintenance and improvement.

In late 1997, as the park was finally being reopened, I first made contact with several members of the FANS group who were cutting brush in an area of the encampment that had been overgrown as long as anyone could remember. I was teaching in the local high school and had developed a course in local history that was narrowly focused on the history of the towns of Easton and Redding, the towns the school served. An important part of the curriculum of that course consisted of the effect that the Revolution had on this area and specifically the impact that the sudden influx of 3,000 revolutionary soldiers had on a town that numbered fewer than 1,500 during the encampment winter of 1778–79. I had also developed a course in anthropology and devoted the first several units to archaeology. As part of those units, I had maintained an archaeological field school that excavated several historic and prehistoric sites throughout the central Fairfield County area. The natural congruence of both of these obsessive interests made a sharp stimulus and spur to action on the suggestion that we conduct some archaeology in the park, put forth by Harry Gibson, a FANS member.

With the backing of FANS, I contacted Connecticut State Archaeologist Nick Bellantoni, with whom I had worked before, and suggested that we be allowed to conduct a limited excavation of an enlisted men's hut to see if the area that had just been cleared of brush was as unaffected by park landscaping as it appeared. In a single fall season, we proposed to establish the integrity of the north end of the site and determine if enough artifacts and features could be recovered to create new displays for the park museum. This was to be primarily an educational opportunity both for my students and for the general public who walked through the park regularly. Those who frequently walked their dogs could and would see how archaeology was done, which, we hoped, would raise the visibility of the park as a historic site and generally stir local interest in the Revolution. David Poirier of the Connecticut Historical Commission, who had excavated in the park in the 1970s, was enthusiastic, as was the state archaeologist, and that enthusiasm spread to the Department of Environmental Protection (DEP), the custodians of the park, and permits were issued that allowed us to begin work in October 1998.

That initial, limited excavation lasted more than ten years and led to investigations of the cemetery area, which turned out to be a regimental officer's quarters, and to two other neighboring enlisted men's huts, which we excavated to compare with the findings of our first year. The results of these years digging up the park are now laid before you. Together with extensive documentary research conducted during the summers, a new picture of the park has emerged that is substantially different from that of the earlier, late Victorian interpretations. This work has shown us the world of the Revolutionary army in a new way, but even more importantly for us, it has finally given us a coherent story, free of the persistent local folklore, to set before the people of Connecticut.

Acknowledgements

To claim that a work such as this is the combined efforts of many people is trite but true. One who especially deserves recognition here is Kathleen von Jena, who joined me during the first season of excavation and stayed with me for six years, serving as the co-director of fieldwork for many of those years. She also became a valued companion and researcher as we visited the sites of other winter encampments and archives containing precious primary information on the Redding camps. Without her help, this work would have been much less complete and minus some major insights. Her encouragement led to the continuation of our excavations so much further than originally envisioned.

The members of Friends and Neighbors of Putnam Park, besides helping to get the process of research and excavation started, were copious in their encouragement and continuous in their curiosity and support. I especially want to thank Harry Gibson, not only for his initial suggestion that the archaeology should be done but also for his continuous help, support and interest. In addition, his willingness to join our field crew and help us dig was always welcome. Similarly, Jeanine Herman, a major force in the formation of FANS, got her hands dirty and continued to support the work that enhanced our knowledge of the park she loves so much.

I also want to thank Carol Franson-Serra, who as a former student had worked on a prehistoric site with me long before the park excavations began. She has become a good friend, and her talented artistry produced the drawings of artifacts and maps that have so enhanced this work. In addition, her encouragement and interest in this writing project were vital to its successful completion.

Thanks are also due to the numerous students who cut their archaeological teeth in the park's trenches. I especially thank those who decided that digging in the dirt can be fun and stayed in the field far beyond the required weekend, in some cases going on to get degrees in archaeology and related fields. Very special thanks are owed to Diana Lynn Messer, who stepped in to take charge of the last season that we were in the field. She capably organized the college students who had joined us that season, and I will be forever grateful for the time she put in even while working on her own college courses. I also wish her good fortune as she pursues a career as a bioarchaeologist.

Thanks are also due the staff of the park for their support, help and interest. Special thanks go to Vincent Masero, who as superintendent of the park when it was reopened in 1997 was responsible for rehabilitating the neglected facilities, but he also saw to it that our needs were met as we broke ground in the park for the first time. In like fashion, I thank Nathan Hale, whose name destined him to be the superintendent of this park. His encouragement and help made the continued excavations in the enlisted men's hut possible. I also wish to acknowledge here the staff of the Connecticut DEP who handled the special use permits and other official paperwork, without which the excavations could not have been conducted.

In any account of those who are to be thanked for their help and support, names are inadvertently left out or are overlooked as the memory of the author ages. This in no way diminishes the gratitude I feel for helping and being part of the process of uncovering, both figuratively and literally, the real winter encampment that was built in Redding in 1778. I hope that you will frequently join me as I lead the annual Winter Walk in the park on the first Saturday of each December, during which we can reminisce and commune with the ghosts of those who went before us into the park.

CHAPTER 1

The Process of Winter Camping

Sergeant Major John Hawkins was exhausted. It was December 2, 1778, and he had begun the day marching from southern New Milford with the rest of Hazen's Second Company of Canadian Volunteers. They passed to the east of the village of Bethel and finally stopped in a densely wooded valley on the Bethel-Redding boundary. His tent was hastily pitched in the manner prescribed by army orders, and he slept that night in the place that was to be home for the next four months.[1]

That same day, Lieutenant Colonel Henry Dearborn entered the same valley. His wife had died in New Hampshire a little over a month before, and in what he described as a melancholy frame of mind, he rejoined the three New Hampshire regiments under General Enoch Poor in Danbury on a rain- and hail-sodden November 30. The next day was spent looking for hutting grounds. That evening, he located the valley that he entered along with Hawkins. His tent was to be on a hill overlooking the rest of the camp since he would be the commanding officer there for most of the next five months.[2] By December 4, everyone was occupied with laying out the camp, and the process of cutting timber used to construct the log huts began almost immediately.

To the modern reader, this behavior is a little strange and is not coincident with the modern picture of warfare. It was the middle of the American Revolution. Why were these troops building winter huts rather than maneuvering to positions from which they could launch an effective attack against the British army? Most mysteriously, why were they camped in the northern half of Redding, almost tripling the population of a small town that had virtually no military value?

Lieutenant Colonel Henry Dearborn, on-site commander of the New Hampshire and Canadian troops at what would later be Putnam Memorial State Park.

The answers to these questions are buried in the earlier history of the Revolution. This military trend to permanently camp during the winter created an episode of the war that lacked national significance but that had such a traumatic effect on the area of western Connecticut that it generated folklore that would be told and retold down to the present. Now this folklore is considered ancient history to modern schoolchildren who play in the park that commemorates the entrance of Hawkins and Dearborn into that wooded valley.

THE CONTINENTAL ARMY AND THE REASONS FOR WINTER CAMPING

The need for a competent army became immediately apparent after the beginning of hostilities at Lexington and Concord in April 1775. Within the next two months, the Second Continental Congress had declared that the forces then gathered around Boston would constitute the Continental army and that George Washington would be the commander of that army. It is one thing to declare a body of men to be an army; it is another thing entirely to turn that body of men into an effective fighting force. This became glaringly apparent when Washington tried to do that with the highly independent men of the New England militia who had responded to the Lexington alarm.

The militia was a colonial institution that had evolved out of the need for defense of the earliest settlements, first against the threat of Indians, both perceived and real, and then the threat of European powers such as France and Spain. According to the early colonial laws, every male between the age of sixteen and sixty was expected to join the militia company for his town or section of town. He was to supply his own flintlock, bayonet and cartridge box. The colony would then supply lead and powder, which would be stockpiled as defensive needs materialized.

The militia members were expected to train regularly, but that training was rudimentary at best. The New England colonies declared at least four training days a year during which new members were given the basics of marching and maneuvering, as well as loading weapons in a somewhat synchronized fashion. These days were even more important as a holiday. In an era when there were almost no public holidays, training days were days free of work during which the citizens of the town would be able to socialize. Women and children accompanied their training fathers, husbands and brothers, usually bringing food for an afternoon repast.

Late afternoons were a time to tend to company business. Among the most important items of business was the election of officers. Noncommissioned officers, corporals and sergeants, served as soon as they were elected. Commissioned company officers such as ensigns, lieutenants and captains, once elected, were submitted to the colonial assembly for approval. One they received the approval or commission paper from the assembly clerk, they served as local company commanders. On a higher level, majors, colonels and generals were chosen by the General Assembly, often at the suggestion of the governor, and served as commanders of the companies as they were gathered into regiments. The general was the overall commander of the colony's militia.

The election of officers was a crucial factor in the development of colonial democratic attitudes, especially those in New England. It also created tremendous independence among the various companies. The company members were responsible to their duly elected officers and only slightly less so to the regimental officers. Each man owed no allegiance to officers from another colony.

As Washington took command, then, he was faced with a group of zealous but undertrained farmers, serving their own commanders and for a limited time. Limited time would be a critical factor leading to the eventual formation of a competent army. When a militia levy was made for a specific defensive purpose, the men signed for a specific period of time, at the end of which they were free to leave and go home. For immediate threats such as that at Lexington, the enlistment time may only have been a few days or weeks. For longer campaigns, such as the invasion of Canada that took place late in 1775, the enlistment might be for six or nine months or even a year. They were never longer than twelve months because it was assumed that the danger could be dealt with in that length of time. The concept of a long-term war did not enter into militia thinking.

The limits on enlistment were essentially a disaster. At the siege of Quebec, for example, the final assault on the city was begun even before the besiegers were ready. As the end of 1775 approached, the commanders, Generals

Richard Montgomery and Benedict Arnold, realized that the New England militia companies were due to be discharged on December 31. Knowing that regardless of the military situation they would begin marching south on New Year's Day, they launched a premature attack beginning at 5:00 a.m. on the last day of December. Within minutes, Montgomery had been killed and Arnold wounded. At least 60 men had been killed and another 426 taken prisoner.[3] Arnold tried to maintain a loose siege into the new year but was eventually forced to retreat back to Lake Champlain.

The magnitude of the disaster created by short-term enlistments was magnified by the loss of veteran troops for the next fighting season. At the end of 1775, up to half of the army had gone home—a great many of these would not reenlist and return for the resumption of fighting next spring. Thus, the commanders were faced every spring with the necessity of enlisting and training a new group of raw recruits, who were poor replacements for the veteran troops of the previous season.

This persistent problem of maintaining the Continental army in the first two years of the war was exacerbated by the eighteenth-century army's habit of not fighting in the winter. There were several reasons for this, the chief of which was the limitations of the weapons of the time. The flintlock suffered from having exposed gunpowder. This was ignited by a piece of flint scraping along a length of steel, thereby shooting sparks into the powder and hopefully setting off the charge waiting in the breech, which was connected to the ignited powder by a small touchhole. If the powder was wet, the weapon would not fire. Thus fighting during the inclement weather of winter was difficult. It was also uncomfortable, especially in the colder winters of the eighteenth century.[4] With European armies generally commanded by members of the aristocracy, who never enjoyed being uncomfortable, it is understandable that war in Europe went on hiatus during the winter months, a habit that was transmitted to fighting in America.

Winter fighting was not impossible, as the Continental successes at Trenton and Princeton in Christmas 1776 showed. The attacks, however, were considered uncouth by the more refined (but defeated) British forces, and after prisoners were arranged for, Washington marched his troops to Morristown for the rest of the winter.

Congress finally came to grips with Washington's perennial problems of forming and reforming an army in 1777 when members finally reorganized the American forces. They passed the "Eighty-eight Battalion Resolve," which ordered the individual states to raise regiments in proportion to their populations. Thus, Connecticut was responsible for eight regiments to create the Connecticut Line, and New Hampshire, a much smaller state, was responsible for three regiments. All eleven of these regiments occupied the Redding winter encampment in 1778–79.

The troops recruited for these regiments were signed up for either three years or the duration of the war. This effectively eliminated the problem of the army dissolving every fall, but it created another problem in that a larger number of men had to be supported in the same place during the winter. The first winter encampment of the new army was Valley Forge. However, the suffering of the troops during this winter, on which modern schoolbooks lovingly dwell, was not created by the severity of the winter, which by all accounts was rather mild, but rather was the result of poor to impossible logistics. In excess of ten thousand men were accommodated at that winter camp, and each one of them had to be fed and clothed for six months.[5]

It was also clear that they needed to be more carefully trained and that army procedures needed to be standardized. That fell to General Frederick William Baron von Steuben, who appeared at Valley Forge in February of that winter. His military credentials have been questioned by historians for decades, but there is no doubt that he effectively brought a knowledge of European tactics and maneuvers to the process of training soldiers. He spent most of that winter dictating a "Manual of Arms" that was used to train the army even as he was dictating it. The effect of his efforts could be clearly seen during the beginning of the next fighting season. At the Battle of Monmouth, the British found themselves no longer facing a ragtag collection of men with weapons but rather a credible army that was able to withstand an assault by the British, who had one of the best armies in the world.

Von Steuben also had an impact on winter encampments. By the time he arrived in Valley Forge, the formation of the huts, the placement of support buildings and the location of the artillery park were already established. He did not directly address future winter camping, but as part of his *Regulations for the Order and Discipline of the Troops of the United States*, he did lay out the proper formation that a camp should assume while on campaign.[6] Thus the enlisted men's tents were to be laid out in rows, with the company officers behind them and the regimental officers farther to the rear. In back would be the baggage wagons, and between the rows of wagons and the soldiers' tents were tents for support services. This same formation would be adopted for the layout of winter encampments, except that the tents would be replaced with temporary log huts that were marginally more comfortable in inclement winter weather. The camps at Redding, coming the next winter after Valley Forge, were the first to establish Baron von Steuben's layout, modified for the peculiarities of western Connecticut geography. This was the situation into which John Hawkins and Henry Dearborn marched at the beginning of December.

WHY WINTER IN REDDING?

The military situation at the end of 1778 had changed since Valley Forge. The British had withdrawn from Philadelphia and had been chased across New Jersey and back into New York City. The center of British military strength had therefore shifted north, centering in New York City and the western end of Long Island. In addition, the British navy controlled the mouth of the Hudson River and most of Long Island Sound. The American forces had also shifted northward to surround the British. Being already situated in this way, Washington decided to deploy his troops for the winter in positions that would allow his forces to keep an eye on the enemy and keep them bottled up in New York. This would also put the American forces into a strategic position to begin fighting the next year, since it was apparent that New York would be the focus of continuing military activity.

The troops were therefore assigned to winter positions strategically placed around New York City. The western flank would winter in Middlebrook, New Jersey (today's Bound Brook). It was also here where Washington and Nathanael Greene, now the army's quartermaster general, established their headquarters. The central position of the American forces would then winter in the Hudson Highlands, where they guarded the approaches to West Point and against a potential British thrust up the Hudson River to cut the colonies in two, as they had tried to do in 1777 before the British disaster at Saratoga. This left the eastern flank in Redding, in western Connecticut, near the military storage depot in Danbury.

Danbury's importance dictated the positioning of the east camps. That town sat astride a major road that crossed the center of the state from east to west. It was located about thirty miles north of the Long Island Sound shoreline, making it relatively safe from attacks from the waters controlled by British ships. Since Connecticut, the "Provision State," was a major source of the army's supplies, this road was vital, as goods flowed westward through Danbury. This made the town a natural depot for the temporary storage of military supplies. In 1777, Danbury also became the location of the area's military hospital when the facilities that had been located in White Plains and Stamford were moved inland to make them less exposed to British patrols.

Its inland position did not render it completely invulnerable, however. In April 1777, General William Tryon landed with two thousand troops at Compo Beach in Westport and, over the next day and a half, marched north through Easton and Redding Ridge and into Danbury. Over the course of the next twelve hours, they searched out most of the stores and destroyed them, along with the buildings in which they had been kept. On the morning of the third day, with the local militia gathering to their south, the British retreated to the southwest, through Ridgefield, where they met heavy resistance from about seven hundred Americans led by Benedict Arnold. The fighting slowed up the British retreat considerably and resulted in a loss of almost 20 percent of their men.[7] Overall, however, the raid was successful in that it had deprived the American army of badly needed stores. The medical supplies were saved, however, when they were moved north to New Milford just as the British were entering the town. This ensured the presence of the military hospital in Danbury in proximity to the winter camps the next year.

The Danbury Raid and Battle of Ridgefield, then, were part of the reason for the placement of troops in Redding. The presence of three thousand soldiers in that location was a powerful deterrent to another raid. Even after the Redding camps were abandoned, smaller contingents of troops wintered in the vicinity of Danbury until the end of the war.

Another benefit of having three battalions of troops in Redding was protection from British coastal and border raids. From the muster rolls kept during that winter, it is apparent that contingents of soldiers were periodically detached "on Command to the coast," where they augmented the coast guard.[8] These were levies from local militia companies and were delegated to spend terms of up to one month in the coastal guard stations protecting the farmers along the shore from quick British raids across the sound. Such guards were especially needed to protect the salt pans in Stamford, salt being a necessary commodity for packing the army's supply of meat.

The Connecticut border with New York was also an area known for raids by groups variously known as Cowboys or Skinners. These were nominal Loyalists and opportunists who raided cattle from the farms along that border and drove them to New York City, where the British paid a premium for them to supply their own troops. Again the muster rolls show several instances in which troops were designated to run patrols into Westchester County to curtail this activity.

Twelve regiments (divided into three brigades), therefore, were stationed in Redding. These troops included all of the eight Connecticut regiments that had been divided into two brigades. The 1st Brigade consisted of the 3rd, 4th, 6th and 8th Regiments, under the command of Brigadier General Samuel Parsons. The 2nd Brigade, then, consisted of the 1st, 2nd, 5th and 7th Regiments, under Brigadier General Jedediah Huntington. Four other regiments constituted the 3rd Brigade: the three New Hampshire regiments that were commanded by Brigadier General Enoch Poor, and the fourth, the 2nd Regiment of Canadian Volunteers, that was commanded by Colonel Moses Hazen.

The combined strength of these three brigades was three thousand men, at least on paper. To ease their impact on the environmental resources such as water, as well as timber for hut building and fuel, the brigades were separated, and each settled in three camps spread across the northern half of the town. The 1st Brigade built its huts in West Redding, and its remains have been entirely destroyed by the building of the railroad and by housing development.

The 2nd Brigade was camped about a mile and a half to the east in a wooded valley roughly on the corner of modern Limekiln and Whortleberry Roads. The above-ground remains of this camp have been partially obliterated by subsequent farming activity, but at least half remains intact. That area has been recently purchased by the partnership of the Town of Redding and the Nature Conservancy and is currently under study by Dr. Laurie Weinstein from Western Connecticut State University.

The New Hampshire/Canadian Brigade was encamped in what is today Putnam Park, about a mile and a half east of the so-called center encampment. This group was technically under the command of Enoch Poor, but at the beginning of the hutting process, he was furloughed, and the command of the park brigades descended on Colonel Hazen.

The brigades were settled in their own distinct areas. The commanding officers, however, were not expected to live with the troops in crude huts. The overall commander of all the brigades was General Israel Putnam. His headquarters was located in a farmhouse on Umpawaug Hill, on the corner of modern Umpawaug Hill and Topstone Roads, which was commandeered for the use of the general and his aides.

The other officers were then sprinkled into other houses about the town. Only a few of the locations of these smaller headquarters are known. General Parsons, for example, is known to have lived on Redding Ridge, on the east side of what would later be known as Black Rock Turnpike, a few doors south of the intersection with Cross Highway. The publication of the Parsons papers has provided some rich details of his work while in Redding.[9] He was involved in Washington's intelligence service and while in Redding lived astride the lines of communication between the American spies and Washington's headquarters, so he remained in residence in Redding until 1781, a considerable period of time after the troops marched out to begin campaigning.

Moses Hazen spent the winter about a mile south of the park in the farmhouse of Colonel John Read—the northern part of Read's farm is where Hazen's troops were camped. According to Read's account book, Hazen rented a room, with another room for his waiter, in one wing of the

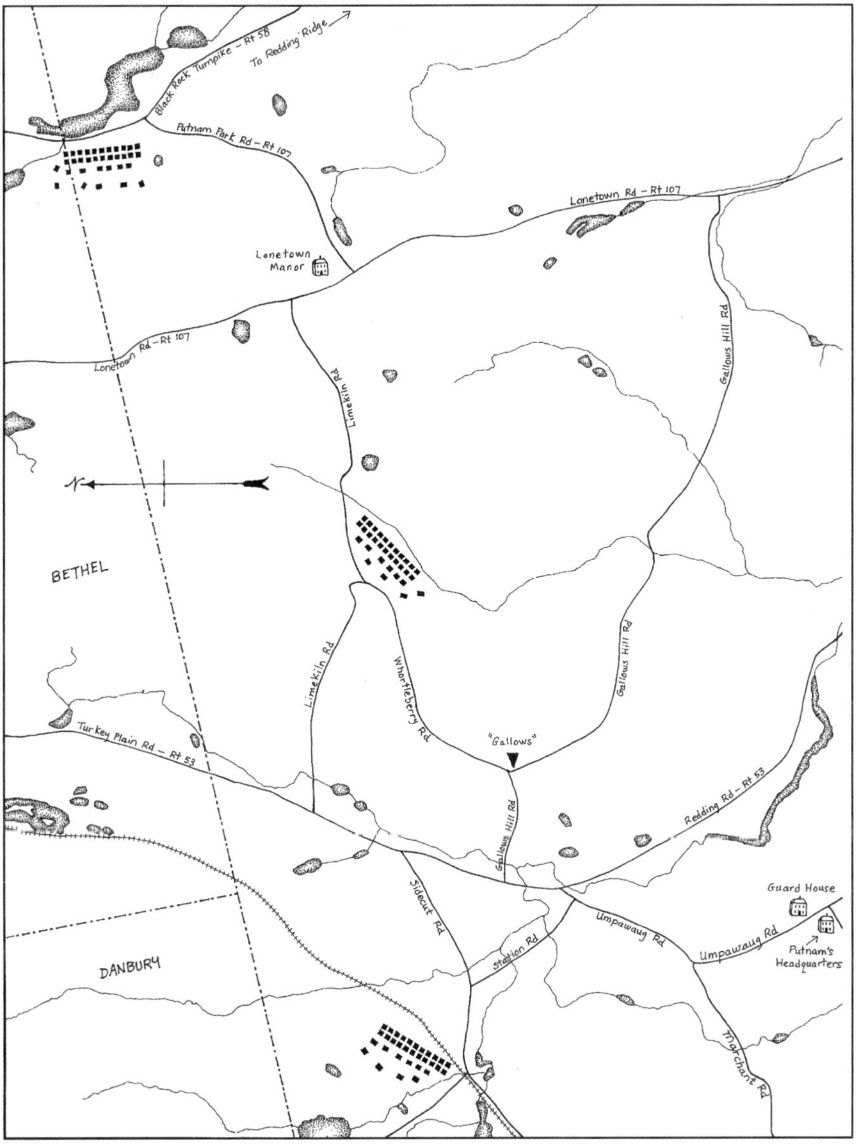

Map of northern Redding showing the layout of the three brigade encampments, as well as Putnam's headquarters and the real guardhouse.

house.[10] He continued to live here until his regiment marched out of camp at the end of March, at which time Lieutenant Colonel Henry Dearborn took command of the remaining New Hampshire brigade and moved from the camp into Hazen's vacated rooms.

The saltbox farmhouse that Putnam used as his headquarters, drawn by John Warner Barber about 1836. It was located on the northern corner of Topstone and Umpawaug Roads.

With the troops distributed across Redding, both Hawkins's and Dearborn's troops began to alter the little wooded valley where they would spend the next several months. As the typical eighteenth-century winter weather arrived, they worked out of their tents to lay out the camps and build the huts that would provide more adequate protection from the elements.

CHAPTER 2

Building a Winter Camp

Both Hawkins and Dearborn had arrived at the hutting ground late in the day on December 2, and the next day was spent setting up tents and engaging in the many other duties necessary for constructing a temporary camp—the one that would be superseded by the more permanent camp of log huts. The next morning (December 4), the troops were mustered, and the brigade orders regarding the precise way that the encampment was to be laid out were read to them.

Hawkins's journal entry for that day reads, "Our Brigade is now busily employed in building Huts for our Winter Quarters; Implements or Tools of various kinds being drawn for the above purpose." Regrettably, subsequent journal entries are missing until January 26, so progress in building the camp is unrecorded. Fortunately, Dearborn—in his typical, laconic fashion—supplied an outline of the activities for that period beginning by echoing Hawkins with his entry on the fourth: "[W]e begin the Day to build Huts."

10th we have a very Sevear Storm of Snow & Rain to day and we living in Tents
11th the weather very Cold, the Snow about 6 inches Deep
12th we are very busy at work upon our Huts, amongst the Snow
13th a very heavy storm of Rain,—& no bread for two days
15th we are covering our Huts
16th we begin to git into our Huts
19th we are in our Huts

The occupation of the huts could not have come at a more opportune moment, for on the twenty-sixth he recorded, "we Have a very sevear Snow Storm," and the next day he noted that "the weather seems more like Canada, then Connecticut."

Dearborn's entries show how quickly a determined brigade of soldiers, suffering inclement weather in thin tents, can construct a small city that would at least partially ameliorate their discomfort. By the third week in December, the camp was substantially complete, and all of the features that can be seen in the park today were in place.

The Layout of the Enlisted Men's Housing

The winter camps were to be laid out in the same way that transient camps were set up while the army was on the march. The process began with the quartermaster staking areas where each hut would be placed, as well as the areas in front and in back of these areas that would supply wood for building and fuel. According to the December 4 brigade orders, "The QM [quartermaster] of each of the Regiments must be Particularly Careful to See the Ground properly Staked out for each Hutt to be built on…The QM of the Several Regiments of the Brigade will Run lines and Mark Trees between the ground both in Front and Rear of their Respective Regiments, So as to secure the wood and Timber properly belonging to Each Regiment."[11]

A description of what came next in the hutting process comes from Hawkins. In his journal under February 11, in an apparent fit of boredom, he gave a detailed description of his surroundings and in the process supplied for us an eyewitness account of the layout he was looking at as he wrote.

In the main section of camp, "the Non-commissioned Officers and Soldiers, with their wives and Concubines reside. It contains One Hundred and Sixteen Huts on a regular Line, Front and Rear, with little vacancy between the Rows like a Lane or Alley. And a similar Space between Hut and Hut as a Passage from a Front Hut to a Rear one." This corresponds nicely with the brigade orders of December 4, which established that "[t]he Hutts to be built in two Rows with 8 feet between them Agreeable to the Established Order of Incamping with Tents."

These descriptions correlate nicely with the visible feature of the park now called the "Company Street," which stretches northward from the monument for 1,500 feet. The piles of rocks that line this "street" are the remains of collapsed hut chimneys, but they have been much landscaped and "neatened up." The first archaeology done in the park by David Poirier in the mid-1970s, however, established that these piles corresponded with eighteenth-century artifact concentrations and were therefore roughly in their original positions.[12] The author's own excavations in the northern part of the Company Street revealed features that were intact, which showed even more clearly that the enlisted men's huts were arranged as ordered.

Today, there are fewer than Hawkins's count of 116 hut remains. According to a 1893 report of the park commissioners, "In the middle of the camp where the field is broader, these stones were carted away within the memory of men now living, and corn, potatoes, rye, and flax were grown."[13] The soil here is poor and subject to erosion, so it appears that the hut clearance was unsuccessful. In the time that David Poirier did his initial 1973 survey, he was able to account for 108 hut remains on the Company Street. The missing four pairs of huts may have been those that were "carted away." A paired pattern of shallow depressions in this bare, "cleared" area may be indications of where the missing hut remains were, but this has not been proven archaeologically.

Eighteen years after Poirier's survey, Ricardo Elias did another survey of park features for the DEP.[14] At that time, there were fourteen fewer chimney remains, and there was a gap in the rows of chimney remains between E41 and E47 and W41 and W47.[15] From interviews with park employees who were working there in the mid-1980s, a section of the Company Street

The southern terminus of the Company Street, which ran north between the parallel rows of collapsed chimney remains. The gravel path to the left is no longer there. The road to the right goes over the parade ground.

was made available to the Department of Transportation for dumping construction debris.[16] It appears that the missing chimney remains were sealed under layers of sand, gravel, loam and asphalt chunks.

The arrangement of the huts in their respective rows was carefully dealt with in the regimental orders: "The huts to be built in two rows with eight feet distance between them." Dealing with the northern portion of the Company Street, where the chimney remains have not been tampered with or landscaped, it was found that the stone remains are spaced twenty-four feet on center from each other. If the hut measured twelve feet wide (east to west) and sixteen feet long (north to south), and the chimney was originally in the center of the west wall, as we established with our excavations (to be discussed shortly), any given hut would extend north from the center of the chimney eight feet and south from the center of the next chimney eight feet. This would leave an alleyway eight feet wide separating a hut from the next northern or southern one, just as the orders dictate. This alley would then allow passage from the front row of huts to those in the rear, just as Hawkins describes.

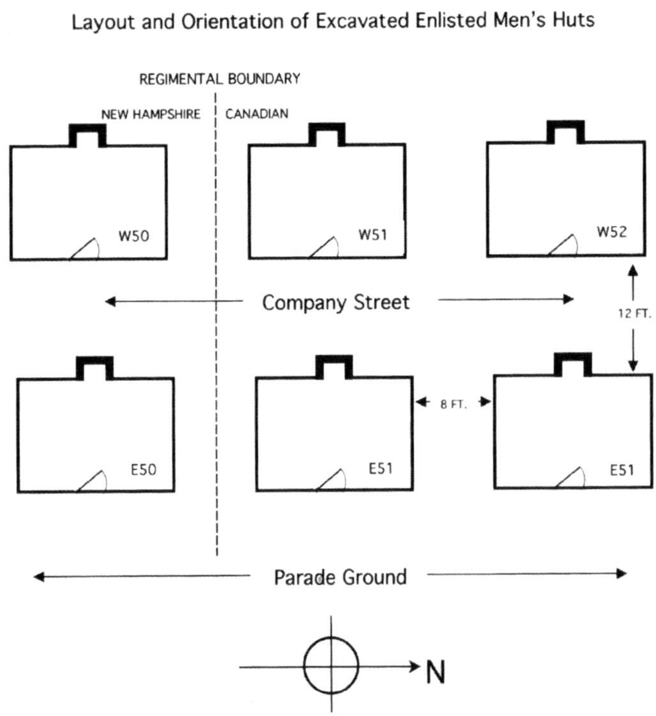

Diagram showing the relationship among the enlisted men's huts that we excavated based on Hawkins's account and the archaeological data we recovered.

Although the orders do not specify the distance between the rows of huts, using the same method of reckoning, that distance can be determined starting with the same twenty-four-foot spacing between east and west chimneys. Thus, from the chimney of the hut in the rear (west), the hut would extend twelve feet toward the one in front (east) of it. This would leave a gap of twelve feet between huts in an east–west direction. This then would be the width of the Company Street, which extended north to south between the rows of huts for their entire length.

The company officers who were in command of individual companies consisted of captains, lieutenants and ensigns, and they were housed in huts laid out behind their companies. Again, according to the orders, "The officer's huts of each regiment must be built in a regular line at about 16 feet distance from the rear line of the soldiers." Since the land slopes sharply upward from the rear (west) of the two lines, it was not possible to place the officers precisely according to the orders. In the area of the present monument, a large rocky outcropping meant that if the officers were to be in a position to supervise their companies, their huts would have to be located on the west

The remains of three chimneys of company officer's huts located just behind the monument, circa 1890. Today, the gravel paths have disappeared, and the standing masonry has been flattened, but they still mark the position of officer's huts, including captains, lieutenants and ensigns.

side of that outcropping, where there are, in fact, three piles of rocks that have been traditionally interpreted as the location of officer's quarters.

Along the main line of huts, there are also occasional piles of rock that appear to be collapsed chimneys and that are located about thirty feet to the rear (west) of the huts. These are not equally spaced with respect to one another nor are they in a straight line, which is probably an accommodation to the very uneven ground in that area. These remains were noted by both Poirier and Elias, but they have not been mapped by either, nor do they appear in the earlier surveys done of the park, even though these carefully noted the locations of the enlisted men's huts. There has also been virtually no archaeology done on these remains that might establish their identity.

Once these hut sites were staked out, a parade ground would have been established. This was probably located in front (east) of the two rows of enlisted men's huts. Such a placement would follow from the location of parade ground in the tent camps prescribed by Von Steuben. The parade ground was the area where soldiers formed up first thing in the morning for muster and where they would drill, so it is an important feature of the camp. Unfortunately, the area to the east of the line of huts is under Putnam Avenue, the gravel access road that was constructed in about 1890 to allow visitors access to the features in the northern section of the park. The extensive grading for the road has apparently destroyed the archaeological integrity of this area completely.

With the huts laid out and construction completed between December 16 and 19, Sergeant Major Hawkins moved into his home and set up housekeeping for the next four months. As a noncommissioned officer, his hut would have been located in the line of huts of the enlisted men of which he was in charge, and thus along the Company Street.[17] His own description of the encampment gives a strong clue to where in this lineup of huts he may have been: "The Bountiful Hand of Providence has given us Water in Abundance. The Land is very Springy. Many has little Springs of Water at the Corner of their Huts, others, near it, and some even at a Corner of their Huts inside." The only place along the Company Street that is this boggy is the north end, and it is undoubtedly at the north end of the line where Colonel Hazen's regiment was billeted, and with them Hawkins. (Exactly where among the huts E51 and W51 through E54 and W54 has not been determined, but based on the usual position of sergeants' tents in the mobile tent camps, it would have been either in the middle of the front line of Hazen's regiment or on its right end, in which case it could have been hut E51.)

This excerpt also gives us a clue as to the water supply for the camp. The northern end of the Company Street ends in a wetland that is formed by the runoff from the hill to the west, which is channeled in a drainage swale that still flows most of the year. This wetland now drains through a culvert into Lake Putnam, but at the time the soldiers were there, the lake was a very large swamp. This drainage swale, then, supplied the soldiers in the northern half of the camp with water.

The southern half of the camp would have resorted to the substantial stream that today feeds Lake McDougal. That lake was created by damming the stream when the park was being landscaped and would not have been there in the eighteenth century, but clearly the stream was draining, as it still does today, the extensive wetland that dominates the southwest corner of the park and beyond.

Another bit of archaeological evidence exists for locating Hazen's regiment at the extreme north end of the camp. While excavating huts E51 and E52,

This shows the enlisted men's hut E50 exposed to the living floor level, including the chinking stones used to weatherproof the sill of the north wall and the large stones that had been removed from the interior and lined up outside the wall.

it was apparent that there had been very little site planning before the huts were built. In both cases, large rocks had been left protruding from the dirt floor into the living space.[18] For hut E50, however, the large rocks had been dug from the floor and placed along the outside of the north wall, in the passageway between the huts. The holes created by removing the rocks were then filled, and the dirt floor was smoothed over, creating a characteristic depression in front of the chimney that was clearly visible even before excavation of that area began. These depressions are also clearly present to the east of the chimney rocks in the other unlandscaped hut sites—thus it characterizes all of the hut sites south of hut E51. Although further evidence is needed, the difference in hut preparation appears to be the result of two different hutting traditions, and it is very likely that the alleyway between huts E50 and E51 is the boundary separating Hazen's Canadian Volunteers to the north from the New Hampshire regiments to the south.

The Layout of the Upper City: Field Officer's Quarters, Auxiliary Structures and a Cemetery

Hawkins's description of the camp begins with an explanation that the camp, or the "City," as he refers to it, was divided into two different sections: "It is something like the City of Quebec, has an Upper and Lower Town and under that Character I shall consider our City." The lower city was the area along the Company Street that consisted of the enlisted men's huts, with the noncommissioned officers, in addition to the commissioned company officers, lodged just behind the Company Street. The upper city consisted of the regimental officers and all of the other structures:

> *In Our Upper Town are the Field, Staff, and other commissioned Officers, their Waiters, with a number of public Huts, such as the Commissary's, the Quarter Master's, the Carpenters, the Shoemakers, the Taylors, the Bake Oven inclosed in a Hut, and the Soap Boilers, beside a hut in each Regiment for the Quarter Guard etc., etc. I cannot give the precise Number, as the Huts are placed so very irregularly and scattered; and the Woods about them not being cleared, I did not take the Trouble to count them; I thought the Labour would be greater than the Curiosity.*

Conspicuous by its absence is the cemetery. This feature does not appear in the earliest records of the park, and it is not until a 1889 commissioner's report that it is mentioned: "On a hill-top, a rude headstone and two or three mounds mark the spot where the bodies of those soldiers who died during the winter were interred."[19] The identity of this plot as a cemetery was formally recognized by the erection of a proper monument and a series of stanchions marking the perimeter of the supposed burial area. According to an article in the *Newtown Bee* dated 1896, "[A] rude boulder monument is erected between the two mounds with the simple inscription, In memory of the unknown heroes buried here."[20] Then, sometime in the 1920s, the plot was surrounded with sixteen granite posts, with a swag chain connecting each to its neighbor. The mounds still remain, but the so-called headstone cited in the commissioner's report has been lost.

Major questions concerning the existence of a cemetery in this area have been raised by Poirier, Elias and myself. Besides the fact that early American burial practices do not include burials in mounds, the bedrock is so close to the surface here that burial at any depth is impossible. In some areas, the bedrock actually breaks the surface, as it does in the western so-called burial mound.

It is known that twenty-seven men assigned to this camp died during the winter occupation.[21] In most of these cases, the muster rolls list them as being "sick in Danbury" just before their deaths, so it appears that anyone

The old cemetery site in 1896 with the so-called burial mounds in the right corner and to the left of the recently placed monument. Upon excavation, these mounds were discovered to be the chimney remains of a field officer's hut.

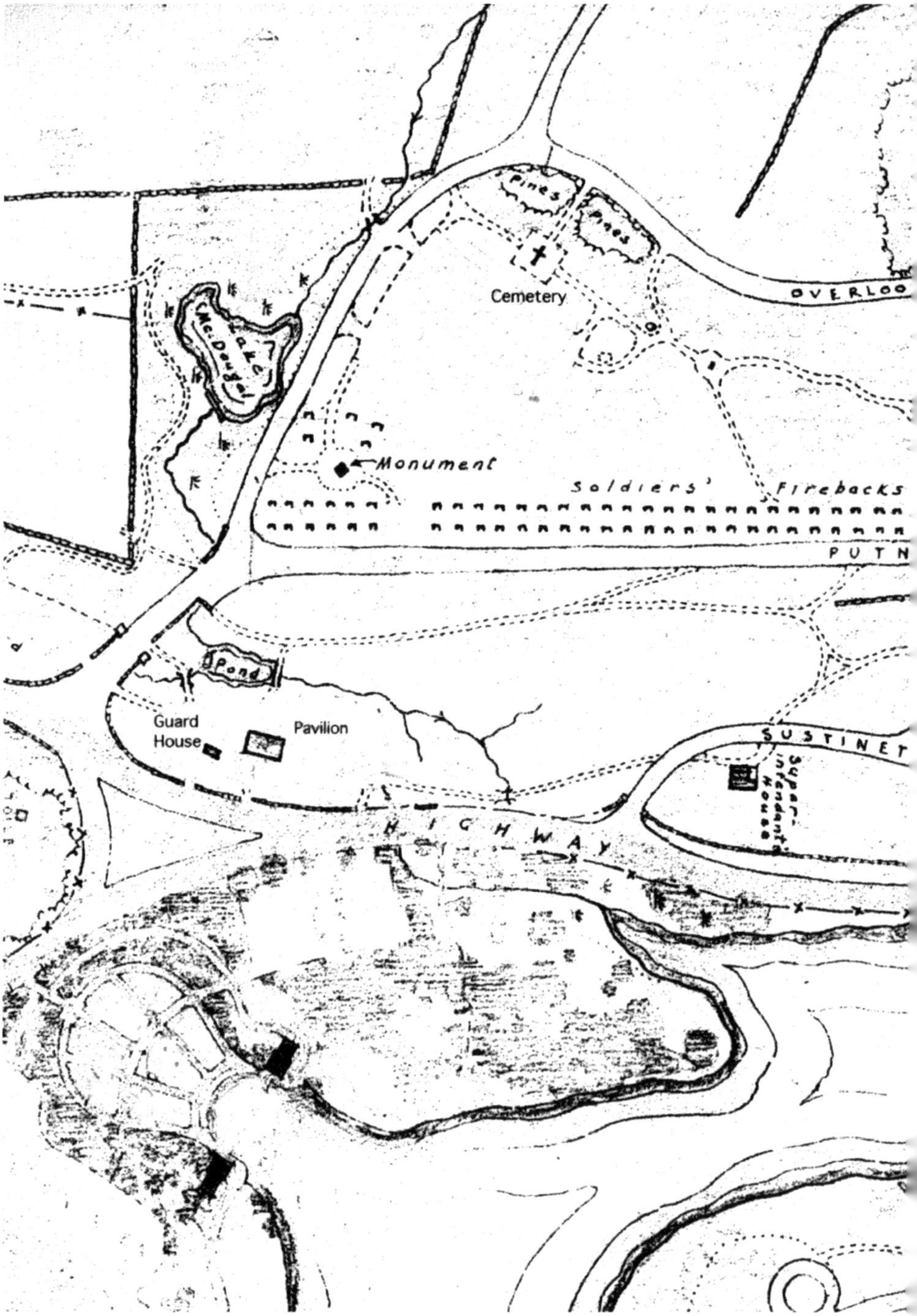

Map of the park done in 1940 to show the principal features of the park.

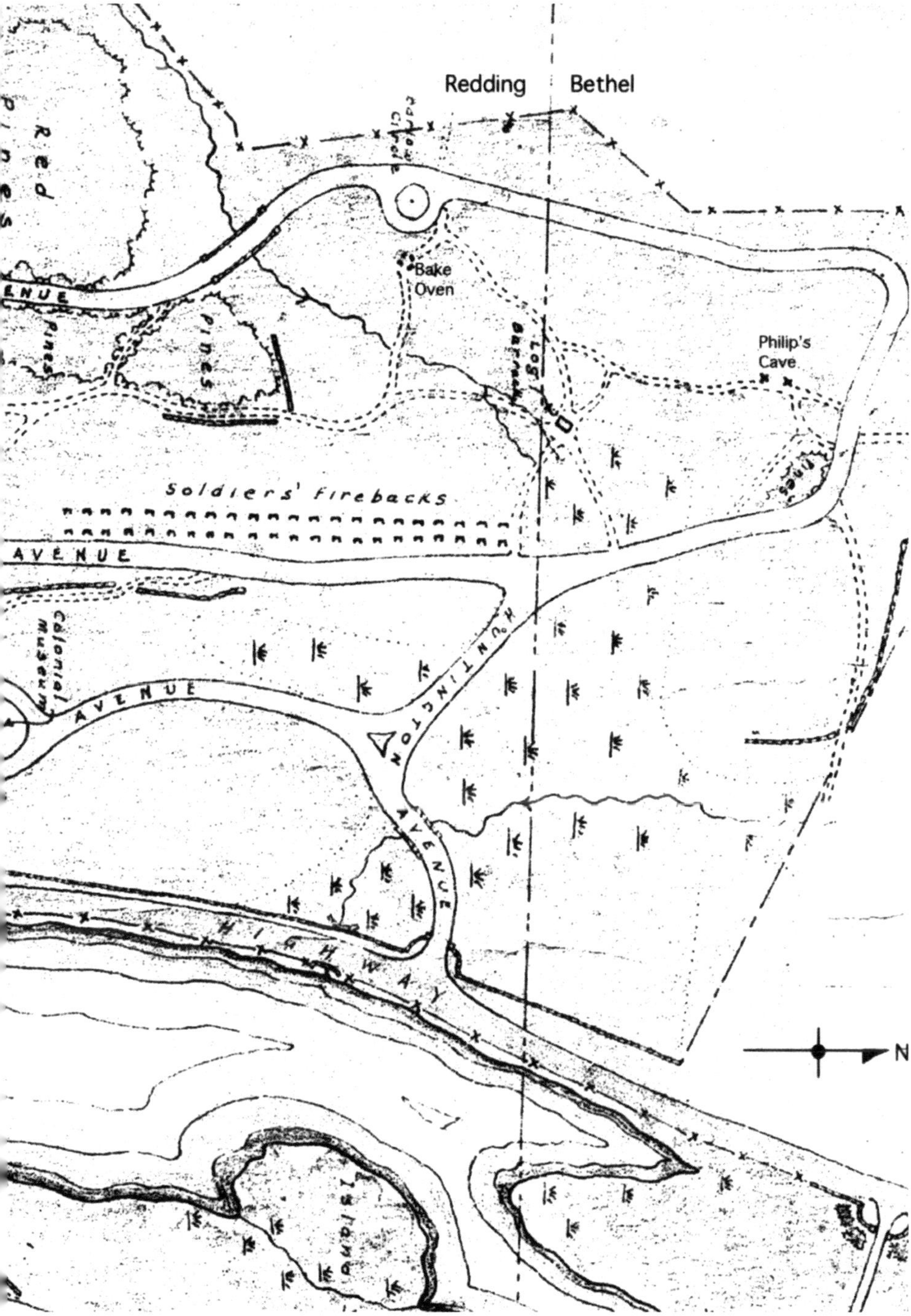
Redding
Bethel
Red Pines
Bake Oven
Pines
Philip's Cave
Soldiers' Firebacks
AVENUE
Colonial Museum
HUNTINGTON
AVENUE
HIGHWAY
Island
N

who was sick unto death was removed to the military hospital that was functioning in Danbury during the encampment winter. If they died there, they were undoubtedly buried in the fields in back of the hospital buildings, as suggested by Danbury's historian, James Montgomery Bailey.[22] It is unlikely that the dead would have been buried on the encampment grounds, where the growing number of grave markers would have had a deleterious effect on the morale of the soldiers. This would also have been the case at other winter encampments, such as those at Valley Forge and Morristown, where no burials associated with the Revolution have been discovered.

To prove that the "cemetery" was not a cemetery and to determine what the mound features were, excavations were begun in 1999 and continued for the next three years. The mounds turned out to be the collapsed remains of two chimneys twenty-two feet apart. Further excavation quickly showed that the cemetery was actually a two-room officer's hut, with chimneys in the west and east wall, typical to the regimental officer's quarters identified in other winter encampments.[23] In reassessing its position with regard to the rest of the camp, and especially the lower city, it became apparent that with the hill stripped of its trees, this was the ideal command position overlooking the rest of the camp.

As the excavations yielded these conclusions, the question of who may have lived in this hut arose. Harry Gibson, an amateur historian with a passion for the park of which he is a neighbor, began a search of the returns of the officers who were associated with the New Hampshire brigades and the Canadian Volunteers.[24] With the exception of Moses Hazen, who was billeted in the John Read farmhouse about half a mile south of the camp, most of the other officers were either on furlough or were detached for other duty. The only officer left in camp was Lieutenant Colonel Henry Dearborn, as is attested to by the muster

Two-room officer's quarters replica at Jockey Hollow, Morristown. Dearborn's quarters in Redding would have looked similar to this but with stone chimneys up to the gables.

rolls and the testimony of his own journal. By process of elimination, then, he must have been the inhabitant of the hut we had excavated.

Regardless of the identification of this feature, the granite posts—minus the chains, which disappeared long ago—and the monument have been left in place. It was the feeling of those who have been so involved in the park that they should be left as a commemoration of the twenty-seven soldiers who died while assigned to the park that winter even though their remains are not in the park.

A metal detector survey of the ground about two hundred feet to the north of what we now refer to as Dearborn's hut resulted in a tight pattern of metal artifacts, which were left unexcavated. There is no obvious collapsed chimney or chimneys nor other identifying features in this area. It is probably not another officer's quarters, but it may be the dwelling and work area of the brigade's quartermaster, a man who worked closely with the camp commander. He was responsible for laying out the encampment, supplying the housing needs of the soldiers and then providing the supplies necessary to sustain the soldiers after the encampment was set up. In Von Steuben's layout of tent camps, the commanding quartermaster is always located just to the right of the commanding officer's tent, so presumably his winter quarters would be next to Dearborn's. In addition, Hawkins's description clearly placed the quartermaster in the upper city. This is, of course, speculation that needs subsurface testing to be substantiated.

The other auxiliary buildings mentioned by Hawkins are undoubtedly about nine hundred feet to the north of Dearborn and the quartermaster, as suggested by the apparent remains of the camp's bake ovens. Hawkins explicitly mentioned that the upper city contained "the Bake Oven inclosed in a Hut"—a so-called bake oven was one of the first features mentioned on the site. It was described in one of the earliest commissioner reports of 1889 and the subsequent 1890 guide to the park as "a circular ruin…the former bake oven." Subsequent guides have also referred to bake ovens on the slope just east of Barlow Circle, although none of those refers to a "circular ruin."[25]

Ricardo Elias, in his 1990 research, plotted the location of the ovens from the 1890 survey map and located an indistinct mound. In the vicinity of this, a one-meter-square excavation unit and six half-meter test pits were dug. The results were not conclusive, but thirty-five fragments of brick were recovered, which argues strongly for the location of the oven on this site or close to it, since brick was not used in any other construction in the encampment. Forty years ago, the author walked this area and distinctly remembers a considerable number of bricks visible on the surface of this area. Today, nothing remains above ground, but there is abundant evidence of erosion down the slope to the east. There is also the likelihood that souvenir hunters made off with much of the evidence.

If the bake oven was in this location, it is very likely that this area was the location of the work areas of the artificers, or "public huts" as Hawkins referred to them. Here, logically, would be the carpenters, the shoemakers, the tailors and the soap boilers. It is probable that they were arranged along the drainage swale that runs down the slope to the northern end of the Company Street since many of the operations of the artisans of this area would have required water. Regrettably, there has not been any archaeology done in this area besides the test pitting done by Elias, so this is one of the least well-known areas of the encampment and remains an area that should have priority in future research.

About the soap works, Hawkins had more to say. Under his extended entry for February 11, he stated:

> *The Soap allowed by Congress being but a small Pittance, and tho' small but seldom received by the Troops, Col. Hazen has erected a Soap House at the left of the Upper Town, and has offered us as an Encouragement to the Soldiers for saving their Ashes, The one pound of hard soap will be given for every Bushel of good Ashes brought to the Works for the first fifteen Days and half a Pound for every Bushel from and after the fifteen Days until the boiler may receive and ample Supply.*

This description gives little evidence with which to locate the soap works since "the left of the Upper Town" is a relative direction. It is of interest that this one work area was known to Hawkins, and it was of enough interest to dwell on it more than the other features of the upper town, which he meagerly described. This undoubtedly meant that he was a patron of the soap house.

One other feature of the upper town would have been an important part of the winter camp. In the extreme northwest corner was a ruin that was described by the early commission reports as "the remains of an old dugout" and as "a stone barrack the sides of which were quite well preserved…it has been restored."[26] The restored hut still stands and is identified as the "Site of Officers Quarters." Although the hut is well behind the Company Street, it is separated from it by a ridge of bedrock and a distance of five hundred feet, putting it into a poor position for the supervision of troops. It is also a dugout, a type of construction that is contrary to the construction methods of other dwelling units in any of the winter encampments. In fact, after the prevalence of illness at Valley Forge, which was attributed to the entrenching

The reconstructed officer's quarters in the northwest corner of the park. Modern scholarship suggests that this was actually the location of the camp's gunpowder magazine.

of the huts below ground surface level, Washington expressly prohibited digging huts into the ground.[27] Since the ruins were of three stone walls surrounding an opening, dug well into the hillside, the structure most likely served another purpose.

The camp's powder magazine has traditionally been associated with a depression directly north of the end of the Company Street and separated from it by the northern wetland. An early mention of this feature in the 1890 guide written by Charles Burr Todd described it as "an old cellar evidently of a magazine or store house."[28] By 1905, this feature was being described in the park literature as the camp powder magazine. This depression, however, when test pitted by Elias, yielded nothing but nineteenth-century artifacts, so it has mostly likely been misidentified.

A far more logical candidate for the powder magazine is the reconstructed officer's quarters. Many powder magazines were constructed into hillsides so that if they exploded, the energy of the blast would be absorbed by the hill. In addition, gunpowder was usually stored as far away from the troops as was practical so as not to endanger their lives. The so-called officer's quarters are located on the other side of a large natural rock outcropping, thus protecting the northern end of the Company Street. The actual location of the powder magazine will forever remain unverifiable since the early park commissioners "rebuilt" the dugout structure, destroying its archaeological integrity beyond reconstruction.

The Guardhouse and Artillery Park

Another case of overzealous park reconstruction was the "guardhouse." This twelve- by eighteen-foot log cabin was constructed about two hundred feet north of the main entrance over existing ruins, which were presumed by the commissioners to be the site of the camp's guardhouse. Actually, the guardhouse for all of the encampments under Putnam's command was located on Umpawaug Road, just a short distance north of the commander's headquarters.[29] It was known locally as the Ephraim Barlow house and was, regrettably, torn down about 1914, but photos of it still exist. Here the offending sergeants would be kept in the aftermath of the aborted December mutiny, and it is also where the two prisoners who were executed in February spent their final hours.

This leaves the question as to what the park's guardhouse ruins were. Since a piece of grapeshot was recovered archaeologically a short distance from the so-called guardhouse, it is very likely that this location may have been the artillery park.[30] This supposition is strengthened by its strategic location. There are only two approaches to the park from the south, the direction from which a British patrol would have to come to attack the camp. The first is over Pocahontas Road, leading down from Sunset Hill, that promontory being the route over which the invading British army passed on its way to burn Danbury during the spring of the previous year, 1777. The second is along modern Route 107. At the time, this was only a dirt track from Lonetown Farm, used by John Read to gain access to his northern acres on which Poor's brigade was camped. If artillery were placed on the knoll where the guardhouse now stands, they would dominate both approaches.

The Ephraim Barlow house, located on Umpawaug Road just south of Topstone Road. It served as the real guardhouse during the Putnam encampment. It was here where Jones and Smith spent their final hours before their executions on Gallows Hill.

We know that there was artillery at all three encampments, used not only for defense but also for signaling in case of an attack. The following is found in an anonymous orderly book for Poor's brigade under the date January 27, 1779:

> *Should the Enemy Advance into the Country the Signal for the Alarm will be in the Discharging of three pieces of Cannon at a Minute Distance from the 2nd Connecticut Brigade* [center encampment], *which will be answered by two fired in the same Manner from Genl. Poor's Brigade after an Interval of Fifteen Minutes, and by two other in the Same Manner from the Artillery of the 1st Connecticut Brigade* [west Redding encampment] *at the Expiration of Fifteen Minutes from Time those are discharged in General Poor's Brigade. In the Consequence of these the several Brigades will immediately parade completely equipped for Action.*

Through a lucky coincidence, we know the identity of the artillery company that was in Redding that winter. Part of the social activities of the officers in Redding was the meetings of the Masonic American Union Lodge No. 1. During the process of recruiting members in Redding, Captain Edward Archibald was inducted on March 17, and in the minutes of that meeting, it was recorded that he was a captain of the 2nd Regiment of Artillery. A search of the muster rolls for Lamb's 2nd Artillery Regiment shows that all of Brown's company had been detached from the rest of that regiment, quartered at Plunkemin, New Jersey, and assigned to the Redding camps. Archibald was an officer in that company. In an unusual footnote to his membership was the further notation that he was "relieved of Lodge Membership" for unmasonic conduct at the end of the very same meeting that voted him entry. He was only a Mason for a few hours, but that was long enough to create a record that allows us to identify the artillery at the Redding camps.

To Build an Enlisted Man's Hut

Both Dearborn and Hawkins set up their tents in the Little River Valley on December 2, and the next day, the quartermaster, while laying out the camp, staked the footprints of the huts that both men would occupy for the next several months. On the fourth, hut building began, at least for Hawkins. Dearborn would have had several enlisted men delegated to build his hut on the hill. Hawkins, on the other hand, had to work with his future hut mates to build their own. Unlike the previous year at Valley Forge, where each brigade constructed its huts in its own distinctive manner, this winter, in the shadow of Von Steuben's regulations, orders were issued with specifics as to how they were to be built, thus making them nearly uniform in their construction:

> *Brigade orders 4th Decr.—78*
>
> *The Hutts are to be built 12 feet by 16 between the joints with the Logs dovetailed together, the Door toward the Brook at one End and the Chimney at the Other. The Square of the Hut must be 6 feet high at least before the Roof comes on. The Gable Ends must be Contracted until they are to a proper point. The Ribbs of the Roof Serving to Shingle upon.*[31]

This order was for the 1st Brigade, located in West Redding, but virtually the same order was sent to the other two brigades as well. It is interesting to see how closely Hawkins's description of the enlisted men's huts corresponded with the orders:

> *The Huts are built with Logs, 12 feet long & 16 feet broad wide. Plaistered* [sic] *with wet Dirt, and covered (i.e. roofed) with Slaps (i.e. shingles): the houses of the Upper Town is the same only the covering which is Boards which is drawn for that purpose. The Huts have all neat Doors fronting to the East, and nice large Stone Chimneys fronting the West and many has Windows. Some to the east and others to the South.*[32]

These descriptions have been largely confirmed archaeologically. The placement of the chimney in the west wall of the huts was quickly established as our first excavations began. Virtually all of the eighteenth-century artifacts were clustered to the east of the chimney and fireplace, which in all three of the excavated enlisted men's huts were clearly defined in the collapsed stonework. The placement of the door was more difficult to determine. In the first hut, we found a slab of rock that was about twelve feet from the center of the collapsed chimney, which could have been a threshold stone, but this is far from certain.[33]

The location of the walls was also difficult to determine because after the huts were abandoned in the spring of 1779, the logs from which they were constructed were salvaged by the landowner. As a result, the sills were removed and not allowed to rot in place, leaving the characteristic soil discoloration that marks the location of walls in a hut that is allowed to deteriorate naturally.

During our first year of excavation, however, we pioneered a method for finding the walls using bone fragments that proved fairly reliable. One of the characteristics of all the park huts that have been excavated is the scatter of bone, usually measuring less than half an inch square, littering the dirt floor. These fragments were the remains of meals that were eaten in the hut. The bone was then walked on and broken into smaller pieces and tracked all over the living area. Since the bone had been in contact with the fire during cooking, they were calcined or dried out, becoming as hard as ceramic shards, which ensured their preservation.

We were all struck by the almost uniform nature of the bone scatter across the floor. This led us to realize that the scatter would have spread to the walls and then stopped. Plotting all of the bone fragments should have showed us the line at which the scatter stopped and thus the position of the walls. Unfortunately, the bone scatter was not just in the huts—the bone had been tracked outside on the bottoms of soldiers' boots, but not in the quantity that appeared in the living area. Persevering, we plotted all of the bones and noticed that there was a definite area where bone was absent. This line of bone-free ground was located just twelve feet from the center of the fireplace, just the distance to the east wall that one would expect if Hawkins's description was accurate and the orders had been followed. The bone-free ground was six inches wide and was effectively the shadow of the sill log. The width of the area further suggested that the sill to the east wall was a minimum of six inches in diameter, or possibly a little larger if some bone fragments wedged themselves under the inside edge of the sill.[34]

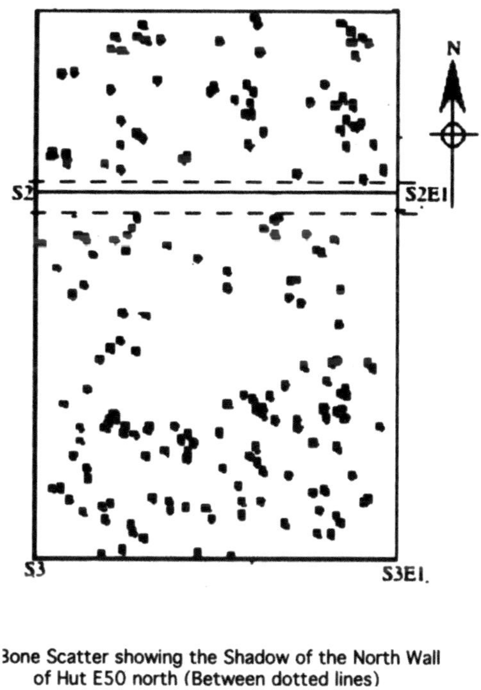

A bone scatter diagram showing the method developed to indicate where the north wall of hut E50 was located. The dotted lines show the wall's shadow. Just by luck, the edge of our excavation unit coincided with the wall.

The bone scatter plotting was extended to find the south wall. A shadow similar to the east wall was found eight feet from the center of the fireplace. This is exactly the distance one would expect if the hut had its long axis of sixteen feet extending to the north and south. We also successfully applied this to the second enlisted men's hut that we excavated four years later. In this case, the position of the north wall was further confirmed by the line of large rock that had been removed from the interior of the hut and lined up against the outside of the north wall. There were also piles of chinking stones that had been forced under the sill to seal the spaces created by a slightly crooked log placed along the smoothed ground. Again, this wall was eight feet from the center of the fireplace, confirming the size of the huts as twelve by sixteen feet.

The floors of the huts were also determined to be dirt. This was not part of the documentation, but we were able to plot the recovered eighteenth-century artifacts vertically, and they all came out at roughly the same level, along with the majority of bone fragments.[35] In addition, there were clear, small fire pits that were dug into the floor, one of which was lined with stone. These pits could not have been dug into a floor that was covered by boards. For most of the area in which we were excavating, this floor level was about six inches below the surface of the ground.[36]

The superstructure of the huts left little in the way of archaeological evidence, but we are blessed with Hawkins's description, which gives us some specifics on the way the walls and roof were constructed. From this, we know that logs used to form the sill of the hut would be laid in a twelve- by sixteen-foot rectangle and that these would be the base of the walls. Roughly hewn logs were then stacked on top of the sills, with overlapping "dovetailed" joints at the corners. The exact nature of these corner joints is not known for certain, but they must have been notched to fit together almost like Lincoln Logs. This would secure the corners and at the same time allow the logs to fit closer together, thus requiring less chinking with small stones and "wet dirt," to use Hawkins's term.[37]

The log walls would have been built to a height of six feet, which would have been the height of the eaves. On the gable ends, the logs would have become progressively shorter until they reached a point. Unfortunately, we do not know by how much the gable logs were shortened in each course, so we do not know the pitch of the roof. The chimneys were also stone built to the height of the eaves (six feet), and then the height of the chimney would have been extended above the peak of the roof with log cribbing—logs crisscrossed and chinked with the same wet dirt as the log walls. This would have allowed the chimneys to draw more efficiently. Samples of the chinking material were recovered from a collapsed chimney of the officer's hut, but to date there has been none collected from the collapsed chimneys of the enlisted men.[38]

The roofing of Revolutionary War winter huts has engendered much debate, but Hawkins left little doubt that the roofs of the Putnam encampments were made of riven slabs.[39] A block of oak or other hardwood would be cut square and about four feet long. Using a mallet and a long bladed wedge with a handle called a froe, the block was split into thin four-foot-long slabs.[40] These were then placed in an overlapping manner on the roof poles or purlins and weighted down with heavy branches, keeping the slabs in place. This type of construction eliminated the use of costly nails. Only four eighteenth-century nails were recovered from the first enlisted men's hut, indicating that the huts were built of interlocking parts, which would have been suitable for temporary quarters. The nails that were recovered were quite probably used for hanging clothes or equipment.

These huts contained twelve men, or two mess groups. According to Von Steuben, six soldiers should be grouped together as a mess or tent group.[41] On the march, these men would pitch a single tent for the group and would receive rations that they would eat together. A winter camp is based on the same thinking: two of these tent groups would share a hut and would receive and cook rations, the remains of which were abundantly evident on the ancient floors.

Given the size of the huts, the living space was cramped. Sleeping accommodations would have been four stacks of bunks, three bunks high. The evidence for this has been taken from work in other camps.[42] The only archaeological evidence of bunk stacks would be post molds, the circular soil discoloration left when the wooden pole supporting the bunk shelves rotted away. These post molds are rare in all of the winter camps in which archaeology has been done. This is probably the result of the posts not having been set into the ground but rather on it. They may also have been removed when the remains of the cabin were salvaged. As the archaeological analysis proceeds, it is hoped that plotting the obviously discarded eighteenth-century artifacts may show how the bunks were arranged, since these artifacts would have been discarded under the bunks and out of the active living area. Regardless of their orientation, there was little room for twelve men to move around one another and their accumulated gear.[43]

To Build an Officer's Quarters

In contrast with Hawkins's hut, Dearborn's was lavish. He would have done little more than possibly supervise the enlisted men who served as his construction crew and those with enough knowledge of dry masonry to construct the chimneys at either end of the building. The most obvious difference was size. Using both bone scatter and the existence of an actual log mold of a sill that remained and rotted in place, we were able to determine that the hut was twenty-two by fourteen feet. This gave him 50 percent greater square footage of living space—that for just two people, himself and his waiter. Although we could not locate any evidence of a partition from the locations of artifacts, we are certain that the hut was divided into two rooms of roughly equal size. This is confirmed by descriptions of other field officer's quarters.[44]

The west room appears to have been Dearborn's private quarters. It contained a relatively small fireplace about two and a half feet wide by two feet deep.[45] The fireplace, in turn, contained some charcoal and the remains of animal bones that were later determined to be the remains of a malnourished goat, apparently the last meal that was eaten in the building.[46] Around the perimeter of the room, more than one hundred hand-forged nails were recovered, strongly suggesting that the room had a board floor. There was also a complete lack of bone fragments or other artifact material in this side of the building that would be consistent with a room that was floored and frequently cleaned. Clearly, Dearborn was leading a more pleasant existence than the men he commanded.

The crescent of large rocks formed the back and right sides of the working fireplace located in the cemetery/officer's quarters. Casting debris was found in the dark soil to the left, and the cooking area was to the right.

The east room of the building was substantially different and reflected a working space where meals were prepared and other routine tasks accomplished. Here there was a clear scatter of bone that was concentrated in proximity to the walls, which is consistent with perfunctory sweeping of a dirt floor. The roughly one-foot area between the fireplace and wall to the left of the chimney held a large number of these bone fragments, making it look as if they had been swept into the corner and out of the way. The relative lack of nails also reinforced the feeling that this room did not have flooring.

This room would have been a public area, where Dearborn would have met with those of lesser rank who would not have been permitted in his private area. It also had a working fireplace, five feet wide by two and a half feet deep. This appears to have been divided into two sections, separated by a line of small stones. To the right was a large amount of charcoal and bone, especially toward the back of the fireplace, where spent fuel and waste bone would have been pushed to get it out of the way of the working fire. The left section yielded small drops of lead, discarded in the process of casting ammunition. Also found here were two musket balls that were about 0.55 inches in diameter. These would have comfortably fit a small-bore pistol, the weapon of choice for an officer.

The large rock is the hearth of the small fireplace that warmed Henry Dearborn that winter. The smaller rocks around the hearth are the remains of the slumped chimney.

In front of the fireplace was a large rock slab, measuring four and a half feet by two feet, that served as a hearth. This rested on the dirt floor, and beneath one edge of it was a broken section of a ramrod about twelve inches long. It was quickly apparent that this had served as a poker for the fire and had been slid under the rock, out of the way but near to hand, when not in use. When the hut was abandoned, this tool of little intrinsic value was left behind in its place of concealment for us to uncover 230 years later.

The exterior of the hut is difficult to reconstruct. It is probable that the logs were covered with boards, for Hawkins noted that "the houses of the Upper Town is the same only the covering which is Boards which is drawn for that purpose." Such a board covering does not leave much in the way of archaeological evidence, especially if the boards were salvaged by the landowner after the camp was abandoned.

The chimneys would have been virtually the same as those of the enlisted men's huts, except that the east one would have been larger. From the scatter of the rock from the upper portions of the chimneys, it is apparent that they both stood for some time after the wood of the hut had been salvaged. At an undeterminable date, they pitched forward, scattering those upper rocks into the area that had been the interior of the hut. This was especially clear in the case of the west chimney, which pitched to the south and east, leaving a distinct pattern of similar-sized rocks in a line from the firebox.

This chimney probably stood about six feet high and was surmounted by log cribbing to bring its height above the roof peak, in the same manner as the enlisted men's chimneys. At the end of the rock scatter was a small pocket of light clay, which was our first sample of the type of chinking material or "wet dirt" that would have been used to fill in the gaps between the logs. Also recovered near the upper course of masonry was a pocket of lime. From this, it appears that the masonry of the officer's chimney was not entirely dry laid in that lime mortar was used to stabilize at least the upper portion of the chimney. Since there are abundant sources of limestone in nearby West Redding, the use of mortar is not surprising, although it must have been used sparingly since very little lime has been recovered in our excavations.[47]

Thus, by December 19, all of these buildings were in place and the camp properly laid out. Both Dearborn and Hawkins now began a daily round of life that would last for four months in Hawkins's case and five for Dearborn. It was mostly monotonous, but occasionally it was broken with special detached guard duty that took them to the coast. It is worth looking at this pattern of living a little more closely since it constitutes the very essence of what a winter camp is all about.

CHAPTER 3

Living in a Winter Camp

With rare exceptions, living in a winter camp is not exciting. It generally consists of a monotonous daily round of activities, interspersed with camp guard duty, drilling and work chores, that keeps enlisted men from being idle. John Cunningham, a respected New Jersey popular historian, recently published *The Uncertain Revolution*, in which he described the winters spent by the Continental army in and around Morristown, focusing on the brutal winter of 1779–80, just a year after the Redding camps. Here, he described the daily life of the soldiers that he distilled from the various orders that were issued on all levels, and the round of activities he sets forward is virtually the same as those for the enlisted men in the Redding camps:

> *Awakened at dawn to the boom of the morning gun. Stand in knee high snow for roll call. Hear the days assignments. Eat a meager breakfast, cooked by a hut mate. Police the camp ground, clean out the latrines or dig new ones, serve officers...Eat dinner (the supposed big meal), a midday time to relax and eat whatever is available. Supper not much. Beating of Tattoo, 8 p.m. bedtime.*[48]

Most of this activity does not leave much in the way of archaeological evidence, although there is still much to discover. The latrines (or vaults, as they were called), for example, have not yet been located. There are orders that these vaults were to be used instead of alternate possibilities that might have seemed more attractive in light of the cold weather.[49] The remains of these undiscovered necessaries, however, can only be deduced from their mention in occasional orders and from the fact that such facilities were essential in any living area.

Other activities can be seen in what they left behind. Hawkins, in his description of the camp, gave an account of the duties for which some of the men were responsible. Among them are "Camp Colourmen, whose duty it is to keep clean the Streets and Alleys in our City." This activity was unexpectedly confirmed by a discovery of a small pile of debris against the west wall of the first hut that we excavated.[50] This debris consisted of six pieces of bone (including a large joint end), four shards of glass, a nail fragment and a piece of lead casting waste. These items do not define a single activity, and all are obviously discarded waste. They were located against the chimney stack at the point where it joined the west wall, a logical place for them to have been swept when the "Camp Colourmen" were cleaning the Company Street. The men doing the cleaning were like any men delegated to military cleaning duties, prone to leaving debris in corners where it would not readily be seen but, in this case, where it would attest to their activities more than two hundred years later.

THE EFFECTS OF WEATHER, FOOD AND CLOTHING ON DAILY LIFE

Daily life in a winter encampment is closely tied with the weather conditions, which determined everything from the level of general comfort to the ability to get food and supplies to the troops. A few years ago, the guides for the park began using the phrase "Connecticut's Valley Forge" to describe the Redding camps. Implied in this comparison was the sense of extreme struggle that every schoolbook history uses to characterize the Pennsylvania encampment regarding its lack of food and clothing and the extreme weather. There was, of course, great suffering, but it was caused as much by the failure of Continental logistics as the harsh eighteenth-century weather.

The Redding encampments, by contrast, experienced fairly moderate winter weather and supply lines as reliable as can be expected in a poorly funded war. Overall, the Redding winter involved little suffering beyond that usual in an army camp. There was frequent snow in December, during which there were seven snow- or rainstorms and four days of notable cold, according to Dearborn's journal, in which he faithfully recorded the daily weather. Then, from January until they marched out in April, the weather was fairly good, with only two snowstorms and one day of extreme cold. On the day before Christmas, he observed that "we had a snow Last night

& very sevear Cold to Day—our men are well Cloath'd and well Hutted," which is a testimony to the conditions being better than at Valley Forge, even in the coldest part of that winter.

There was also a very early spring. On April 2, he remarked that the "weather Remarkably fine for the Season," and on the eighth, he noted that "the weather is very fine for the Season it is said by the old men so forward a Spring has not been known." Two days later, he observed that the peach trees were beginning to bloom. All of this was in sharp contrast to the next winter spent in Morristown, which most historians consider to be the worst winter on record, with logistical problems at least as severe as those at Valley Forge.[51]

Although the Redding winter was not as bad as other Revolutionary winters, it did create problems with food supplies, which were carted to the camps from the supply depot in Danbury. Private contractors hired teamsters, and a number of Redding men signed on with their wagons and teams, including James Sanford, who left a brief account of his efforts in a pension deposition in 1833. He came from the area of Poverty Hollow and worked for four months getting supplies from Danbury to Poor's brigade at what is today Putnam Memorial Park.[52] The occasional early deep snows made his carting difficult, but even more difficult were the late winter thaws that often bogged the carts to their axles in mud. Thus there were shortages that led to General Samuel Parsons's complaint and explanation to his troops in this brigade order:

> *The General of the Brigade informs the officers and soldiers that he has used every possible method to supply flour or bread to the brigade. Although a sufficiency of every article necessary is at Danbury, the weather has been so extreme that it is impossible for teams to pass to that place. Every measure is taken to supply flour, rum, salt and every necessity to morrow, at which time if a quantity sufficient come in all past allowances shall be made up.*[53]

The diet of the average soldier (promised by the commanding officers) is recorded in brigade orders. From the orderly book of Joel Smith, for the 3rd Connecticut Regiment camped in the center encampment, the adjutant's orders for April 24, 1779, claimed that the food that was to be distributed to each soldier consisted of "1 lb ¼ flour, 1 lb. ¼ of Beef or 1 lb. of Pork or 1 lb. of Fish ½ gill of Rice and one gill [¼ pint] of Rum. Only ¾ of lb. of Flour is to be deliver'd for the present & Certificates to entitle the troops to the pay for the remaining quantity."[54] These orders echo the officially recognized diet requirements of the Continental army throughout the middle years of the war and would have applied to all of the Redding soldiers.

The type of food delivered to the New Hampshire and Canadian troops, aside from periodic shortages, was not a problem, but archaeology suggests that the quality of food was. Although bone fragments left from meat that was eaten in the huts were plentiful and ubiquitous, the vast majority were too small to determine what species they represented. David Poirier also reported in the results of his 1973–75 excavations that 98 percent (11,981 pieces) of the Revolutionary War cultural material that he recovered were faunal remains (i.e., bone fragments), while only 3.1 percent (377 fragments) were identifiable as to species, "including horse (teeth) and some small wild species"—this suggests that some hunting was done.[55] He found that there was a lesser quantity of cow, pig and fish than had been reported for the previous year at Valley Forge. He further tentatively concluded that comparing the quality of meat consumed at Redding was dependent on a "narrower inventory of domestic species as well as on poorer quality of cuts of meat."

The lower quality of meat was also reflected in our excavations. We were faced with the same difficulty of identifying animal species, but we did recover recognizable fragments of horse jaw, along with several teeth, scattered in all three of the enlisted men's huts. Using head meat, especially the lower jaw, indicates that a high amount of the protein was not being ingested.

The use of horse meat does not appear anywhere in official army record, but it does in private reminiscences and journals. In the notable memoirs of Joseph Plumb Martin, for example, he described getting settled in the middle encampment: "We got settled into our winter quarters at the commencement of the new year and went on in our old Continental line of starving and freezing. We now and then got a little bad bread and salt beef (I believe chiefly horse beef, for it was generally thought to be such at the time). The month of January was very stormy…and in such weather it was mere chance if we got anything at all to eat."[56]

From this, it can be readily understood why soldiers resorted to scavenging from local farmers, which is reflected in Parsons's general orders of January 19: "Complaints have been made that the inhabitants have suffered great injury by the lose of sheep, poultry, and many other articles since the troops have been stationed at this place. The General cannot suppress his indignation that any of the soldiers under his command should be guilty of such wanton scandalous conduct."[57] This must be the reason for the chicken bones that we recovered, for no poultry is mentioned in the official orders.

Clothing was another area in which the Continental army always seemed to be in chronic short supply. A shipment of French clothing just before the construction of the Redding encampment, however, ameliorated this problem, at least temporarily. As a result of the American victory at

Saratoga, which showed that the American army could defeat British regulars, the French concluded an alliance with the fledgling United States, and this resulted in a trickle of supplies. A French shipment of Charleville muskets was part of this trickle, and most of the New Hampshire men benefited by being equipped with these new firearms. This accounts for the preponderance of .64-caliber musket balls, a size that fit the smaller-bore French weapons, which we had recovered in the enlisted men's areas.

This supply stream, including a large quantity of shoes and clothing, had arrived the previous autumn. The clothing included coats, waistcoats and breeches of uniform colors, except the coats, some of which were blue with red facings and others were brown also with red facings. The differences in color created a problem in that the blue coats were favored by the soldiers, who saw them as the proper Continental color. They were therefore assigned to state regiments by lottery in October 1778, probably held in Fredericksburg, New York, which was Washington's headquarters just before the settlement into winter camps.[58] Four states were awarded the blue coats, and five, including the New Hampshire regiments and Hazen's Canadians, received the brown coats. The average soldier camped in the park area, then, sported brown uniform coats with red facings.[59]

This did not mean that there were not problems with clothing and blankets. The winter weather and heavy-duty activities took their tolls on the uniforms and especially shoes. By the end of the winter, brigade returns claimed that 182 men in Hazen's Regiment were "unfit for duty for want of Shoes."[60] Overall, however, the soldiers of the Redding camps were probably better clothed than they ever had been.

Daily Activities of Enlisted Men

The daily round of activities was basically the same for all enlisted men and ran in the cycle quoted earlier. Activities specific to particular huts are not covered by official orders nor are they dealt with in any other documentation, even diaries. These activities are the domain of archaeology, which recovers the scattered remains of a former living area and attempts to reconstruct the activity that produced those remains and patterned their distribution.

A good example of what archaeology can reveal centers on the large rock that protruded into the living space of the third hut that we excavated (E52). This rock was too large to be easily removed during hut preparation and so was left and apparently incorporated into the inhabitants' living routine. Around it was clustered a pattern of artifacts that indicated activities that

The exposed floor level of hut E52. The large rock to the left is the furniture rock on which a soldier sat while casting musket balls and repairing buttons. The rocks in the upper left are the remains of the collapsed chimney.

centered on the rock, suggesting that it was a "furniture rock" used to sit on while performing activities. Using a large intrusive rock in this fashion would have been logical in that it kept one from sitting on the cold, damp floor, although not by much in a hut in which there was no furniture besides the stack of bunks.

Just to the west of this rock, a small pair of scissors was recovered. It measured about four inches long and was in remarkably good condition given the fact that it was made of iron and had rested in an acidic soil for two centuries. Only the ends of the finger holes were missing. This small artifact was ideal for carrying in a pack to be used for mending clothes and replacing buttons. At some point in the mending process, it appears to have been set down on the dirt floor near the man's boot, where it was forgotten or possibly stepped on, pushing it out of sight, to be recovered by us 230 years later.

As if to corroborate this possible scenario, three buttons were found in a radius of about four feet. These are referred to as "civilian buttons" by military button collectors since they were not used on the uniforms but rather on undergarments that would have been supplied by the soldier himself.[61] They were all similar, being about three-eighths of an inch in diameter and

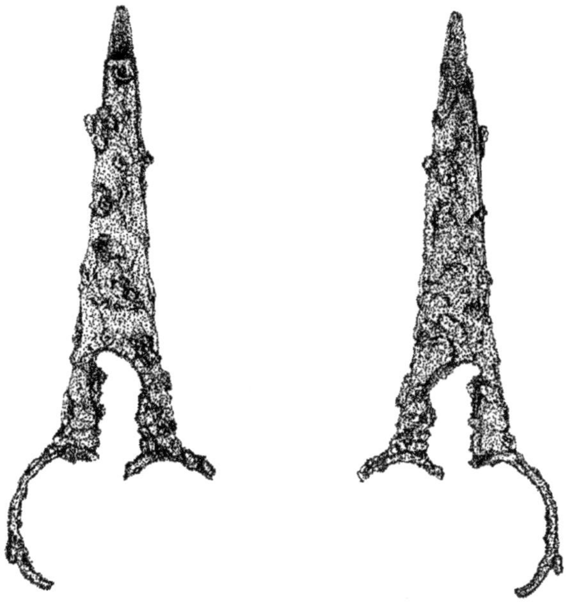

Found just south of the furniture rock, this four-inch pair of scissors was probably used for replacing the buttons also found around the rock. *Drawing by Carol Franson-Serra.*

made of pewter. These discs were actually the backs of buttons, the fronts of which had thin brass coverings that had been crimped around the back. In all cases, this covering had been removed or lost. On two of the backs, the loop that was used to secure the button to the garment was broken, showing the reason for the mending session.

One of these buttons was of unusual interest in that it had four small cavities on the back. These were drill marks, and two of them showed that the soldier had trouble drilling the desired holes since a start had been made but abandoned. The other two succeeded in penetrating the back and would have allowed him to sew it to the garment. For some reason, the attempt was unsatisfactory, and the rejected button found its way into the rubbish on the floor. This discovery, however, documents a primitive attempt at recycling.

Another button discovered in the second enlisted men's hut we excavated (E50) was associated with the area just in front of a bunk. Only one-fourth of it survived, but it had originally been about the size of a quarter. It was made of pewter with a silver wash, and when intact, it had a set of four stylized roses cast around a central rose and a beaded border. What made this object unique was the fastening device. On the reverse, there was a cylinder cast into the back, with a hole running down it parallel to the plane of the back. No

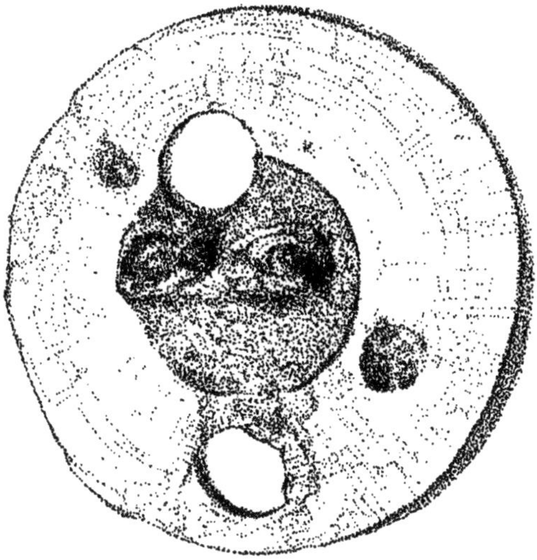

Reverse of the button that a soldier attempted to recycle. The broken loop necessitating the repair is in the center, and two attempts to drill holes are to the right and left. Two successful attempts are above and below the broken loop. *Drawing by Carol Franson-Serra.*

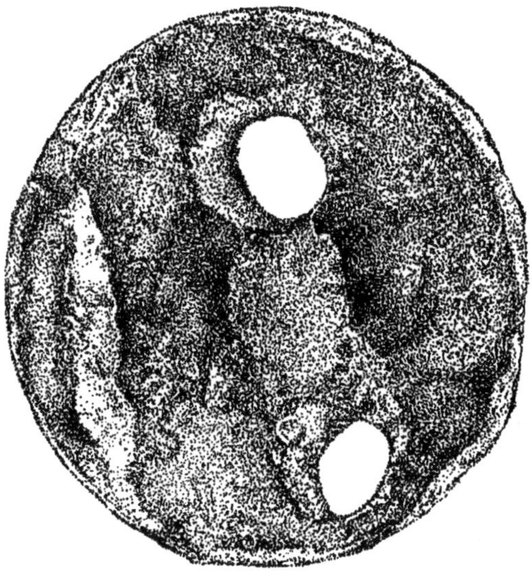

The obverse of the same button, showing part of the broken brass covering to the left. *Drawing by Carol Franson-Serra.*

prototype of this kind of button has been found, and it may, in fact, not be a button at all. It has been suggested by several people who examined it that it is a type of decoration, maybe for a harness. This possibility is strengthened by the proximity of what has been identified as a broken horse bit that was found about a foot away underneath what would have been the protective covering of a bunk. There has been nothing similar to it in the site reports of other eighteenth-century military sites.[62] It still remains one of the park's mysteries.

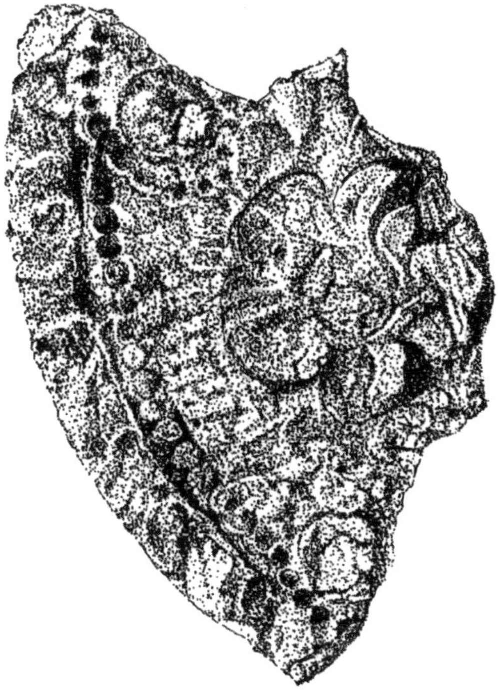

The one-fourth section of the mystery ornament or button, showing the obverse. *Drawing by Carol Franson-Serra.*

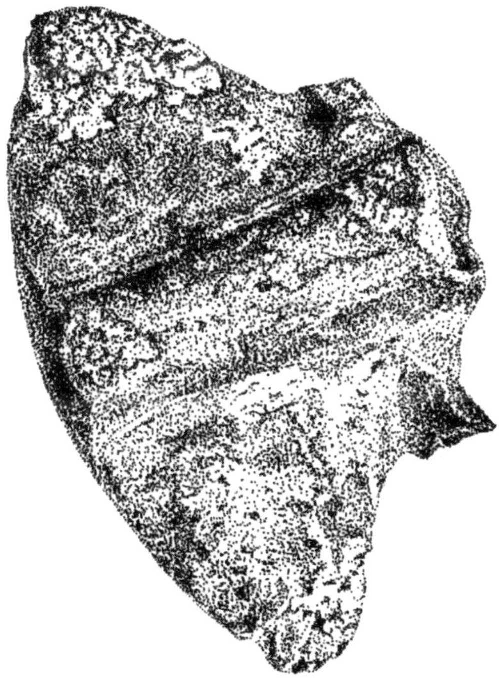

The reverse of the same ornament fragment, showing the small cylinder for attachment running across the center. *Drawing by Carol Franson-Serra.*

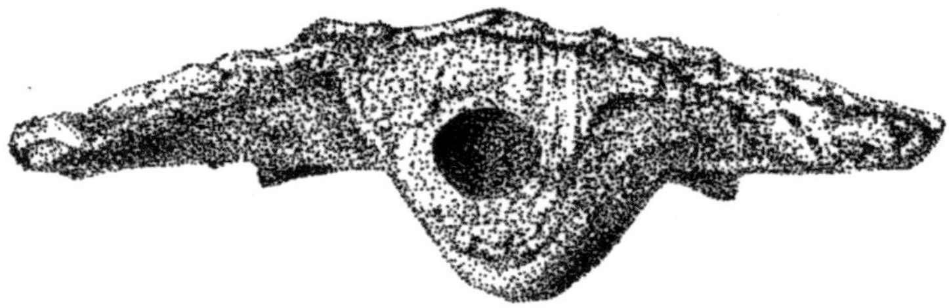

The mystery ornament seen from the side, showing the end of the cylinder used for attachment. *Drawing by Carol Franson-Serra.*

Another activity area was also associated with the same rock used by the button mender. About four inches to the north of the rock was a seven- to ten-inch circle of charcoal that was about five inches deep. It was obviously the remains of a small fire pit located about five feet to the northeast of the fireplace opening. A similar pit had been found in the first season that was a little larger and lined with stones. Nothing in the contents of that first pit gave any indication of its use besides the fact that, for some reason, a soldier had started a well-controlled fire in the dirt floor in front of and not in the fireplace.

Careful excavation of this second fire pit showed us how it was used. Firmly embedded in the bed of charcoal was an unmistakable piece of lead spilled during the process of casting musket balls. As if to confirm our analysis, a finished musket ball was discovered at the edge of the fire pit. There was also a second casting pit just to the west of the first, about four feet to the northeast of the center of the fireplace. This pit was larger, measuring fourteen inches in diameter, and was dug about six inches into the dirt floor. Its presence and the possibility of a third pit to the south of the second strongly suggest that the casting activity in the hut was a repeated process. The possibility that three men were casting at the same time seems unlikely since these pits were so close together that they would have interfered with one another to the extent of inflicting burns or even just disrupting the casting process.

The placement of these casting pits poses a mystery. Most logically, casting would have been done in the fireplace, where there was already a fire and where the smoke would be drawn up the chimney. Why cast on the floor five feet away from that fireplace, where the smoke would have risen into the hut, befouling the air? This remains an unanswered question, although the smoke may have not posed such a problem since the roof boards were loose and probably not weather-tight. The smoke may have just vented around the boards if there was not heavy snow cover on the roof, sealing it. Is it possible that casting was just done in the early spring just before the troops departed for the coming campaign season? This would have been a time when the hut was snow-free and would have allowed smoke to rise and pass out though the porous roof.

The size of the musket ball recovered from the edge of the casting pit is also a clue to the type of weaponry being used at this point in the war by both the New Hampshire regiments and Canadians. That ball, as were the majority of others that were recovered in the park, measured 0.64 inches in diameter. This size was specific for the French Charleville musket, which had a bore of 0.69 inches. (The common British Brown Bess musket had a larger bore of 0.75 inches and used a ball measuring 0.69 inches.[63])

It is well known that some of the French aid that seeped into America after the victory at Saratoga in 1777 was in the form of French weapons, consisting mostly of the Charleville musket. Most of these were distributed to the New Hampshire regiments early in 1778.[64] It is not surprising, therefore, that the bulk of ammunition recovered would be that suitable for French firearms. Since those that were discovered in what we feel strongly was the Canadian section of the encampment were also of the smaller diameter, it seems likely that the members of the Second Canadian Volunteers were also the recipients of the French bounty.

Artifacts recovered from under where the bunks would have been also revealed something about the handling of discarded waste, the recovery of which yielded more information about the daily life of the enlisted men. The simple fact that refuse was unceremoniously pitched under a bunk to get it out of the way comes as no surprise in a company of men whose housekeeping chores were far from fastidious.

The discovery of a single brick among this refuse, for example, was revealing in that it hinted at a heretofore unsuspected nighttime practice. The brick was an eighteenth-century handmade brick. In brick collecting parlance, it was a soft paste brick, meaning that it had been fired under a low heat and therefore was soft and easily broken. We had been recovering small, unglazed shards of what we thought was unglazed red ware pottery scattered on the old floor level. They were not recognized as brick fragments until the concentration of large fragments was recovered and recognized as brick. From the shattered nature of this concentration, it became clear that the brick had been heated, probably in the fireplace, and that at one point residual moisture in the brick rendered it into the fragments that we recovered.

The question it immediately raised was why a single brick was recovered from within one of the huts. It obviously did not have any architectural

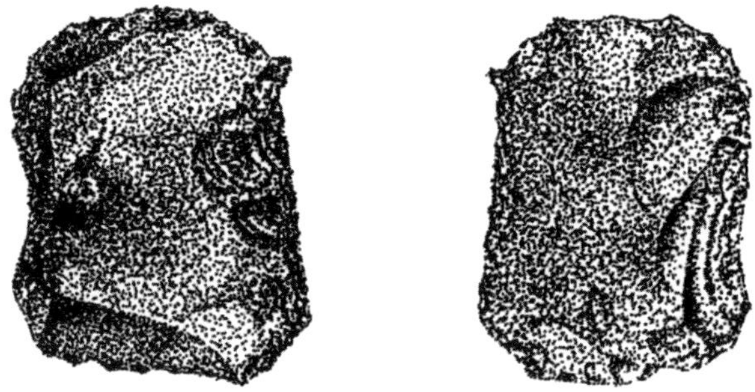

Gun flint typical of the ones used on the New Hampshire soldiers' muskets. This one is no longer usable and was discarded—to be found by us under where a bunk stack would have stood in hut E50, more than two hundred years later. *Drawing by Carol Franson-Serra.*

function. A logical possibility is that it served as a primitive bed warmer. Once warmed in the fire, it would have been tucked under the blanket with the soldier as he lay on the bed of straw lining the boards of his bunk. If this is the case, we came upon the first indication that soldiers practiced a means of keeping warm away from the radiant heat of the fireplace. Fragments of apparent red ware have also been uncovered in other huts, and these may be an indication that the practice was not unique, but so far, no other large, obvious brick pieces have been found.

Another class of artifacts was recovered from the first enlisted men's hut we excavated (E51), and it shed light on a practice that had previously been hidden in the orderly books. Under the bunks that would have been located in the southeast corner of the hut were two broken glass pharmaceutical vials, obviously thrown there to keep the inhabitants safe from being lacerated on the broken edges. Such vials are not known to have been recovered from any of the other huts, so their unique appearance here was initially a mystery.

The reason for their presence may lie in the orders issued to the regiments shortly before the camp was abandoned: "The Officers of the Division are most earnestly Called upon by the Gen'l to See the no injury is done to the Hutts which are or may be evacuated, that neither the door, laiths, floors or any part of them are destroyed so as to prevent them being converted into Hospitals or any other purpose for which they are proper and may be used."[65]

The key word in this quote is "hospitals." From the muster rolls, we know that at every roll call several men would be accounted for by being listed as "Sick in Camp," which meant that they were too sick to be on duty but not so sick that they needed to be taken to the military hospital in Danbury. Those who were too sick to march out of camp with the other members of their regiments in the spring would remain behind until they were well and able to rejoin them. The reason for Putnam's order, therefore, was to allow recuperating men to be consolidated into one of the preserved huts and cared for more efficiently.

From the time that we excavated the second enlisted men's hut, it was apparent that we were recovering many fewer artifacts, especially the fragments of bone that had seemed to be so plentifully scattered on the floor of the first hut. This strongly hinted that the first hut had been occupied for a much longer period of time than the second or even the third hut. This would have been the case if sick soldiers, left behind at the time of evacuation, were concentrated in the first hut, where they remained until they could rejoin their regiment. The presence of two pharmaceutical vials strengthens this speculation considerably.

Not all refuse was found under the bunks. In the second hut (E50), two artifacts were recovered just in front of the bunks, where a soldier would have set his feet upon getting up or even just using the bunk as a seat. One was a broken fragment of the outer edge of a shoe buckle. It was made of brass or bronze and was remarkably thin and delicate. Decorated with a badly corroded ropelike or chordlike design, this was a remarkably ornate bit of adornment for the shoe of an enlisted man. It is little wonder in the rough life of a wintering soldier that the edge became bent and eventually broke off from the resulting metal fatigue. It then appears to have fallen to the dirt floor at the side of the shoe and was lost after being stepped on and pushed into the dirt.

Next to the buckle fragment was a brass clip that at first resisted identification. A British reenactor waiting for a mock skirmish to begin during the weekend of its discovery readily identified it as a clip for a bayonet scabbard, used to attach that scabbard to the soldier's belt. He excitedly pulled his own replica scabbard from his belt to show us the clip as it would have originally appeared in use. It was identical to the one we had just excavated. He further informed us that this piece of personal hardware was frequently pulled free from the leather scabbard as a result of the stress placed on it as it was worn.

Even more exciting to all of us was the small piece of leather from the original scabbard that was still clamped firmly between the clip and its backing plate. Virtually no soft material survived in the moist soils of the park. This fragment of leather had survived because it was clamped between two pieces of copper alloy. The salts created when copper corrodes are poisonous to the bacteria that would have destroyed the fragment of leather, thus preserving it.

We are not sure where Sergeant Major Hawkins's hut was located, but according to the established order of camping, his hut should have been at the south end of the line of huts occupied by Moses Hazen's Canadian regiment. That would have placed it in the general vicinity of the three huts that we excavated. Even though he was the highest-ranking noncommissioned officer in the Canadian regiment, he would have lived with the enlisted men under his command and not in the huts behind the Company Street reserved for the company officers, the captain and his subalterns. Therefore, Hawkins's daily life would have been very much the same as that described above with few if any privileges.

DAILY LIFE OF THE REGIMENTAL OFFICER

The daily life of Lieutenant Colonel Henry Dearborn was radically different from that of Hawkins. This was most apparent in the placement of his quarters, above and far behind the Company Street, and in the substantially greater living space that he and his waiter (or servant) enjoyed.[66] Compared to the 192 square feet of an enlisted man's hut into which twelve men were crowded, Dearborn enjoyed 308 square feet for just himself in his own room and his waiter, who probably lived in the other room to be available at Dearborn's beck and call. The presence of such a servant also suggests that the cleanliness of his living quarters was substantially greater than Hawkins's. This seems to be born out archaeologically. There were virtually no bone remains nor any other refuse associated with the area that corresponded to his room. This would certainly have been the case if he had a board floor that was frequently swept clean.

The only piece of refuse that was recovered from Dearborn's room was the joint end of a sheep femur. While examining this a short time after its recovery, Connecticut's state archaeologist, Dr. Nicholas Bellantoni, noticed that its surface was marked by small carnivore marks. The bone had apparently been chewed on, most likely by a small dog. This small piece of evidence reinforces the reasoning that this was Dearborn's dwelling, since he was known to have kept a dog throughout his service in the Revolution. In fact, the dog he had during the ill-fated invasion of Canada in the late fall of 1775 became the subject of notoriety in several journal entries, including those of Dearborn himself. Because of severe logistical miscalculations and mistakes, as the troops reached the headwaters of the Kennebec River, they found themselves without rations and starving. As the situation became critical, Dearborn's dog was sacrificed in the cooking pots of a number of his troops. It is of interest that the dog he had with him in Redding was a small lap dog, based on the separation of the canine teeth marks.

Although the evidence is scant, it does indicate that a better diet was enjoyed by Dearborn while he was in camp. The bone remains found in his fireplace, which were certainly part of the last meal that was eaten there, was that of a malnourished goat. This does not appear to be particularly sumptuous, but it was at least fresh meat, something that appears to have been a rarity among enlisted men.[67]

There is also the evidence that he enjoyed fresh shellfish on at least one occasion. In his journal for January 22, he noted, "I went to the Sound for Oysters," and the following day he "[r]eturned from Norwalk."[68] This twenty-two-mile trip may have been made for some unrecorded military business, but he was moved to only record the acquisition of shellfish. He also appears to have brought back some to enjoy in camp because in the corner of the waiter's room, where most food would have been prepared, we recovered a small quantity of clamshells. Given the eighteenth-century lack of precision in referring to shellfish species, these quite well may have been Dearborn's oysters. Regardless, they indicate a food source that the common soldier did not have the freedom of movement to acquire.

Ceramic shards were also a high status marker for Dearborn. The only indication of ceramics in the enlisted men's huts were crude red ware pottery shards, which were often unglazed or at most glazed in black with an occasional light-colored stripe. In the workroom of Dearborn's quarters, three pieces of white porcelain with hand-painted blue designs were recovered—in the lab, they were found to fit together into one large fragment. Its shape led us to believe that it was a sugar bowl, a small pitcher or some other piece of an expensive tea set that was clearly beyond the financial capabilities of those of lower rank.

Unexpectedly, we also found evidence of lead casting, a mundane activity that we assumed was characteristic of the lower ranks. The large fireplace in the workroom had been separated into two sections by a distinctive line of small rocks. The right section was obviously used for food preparation and contained a large amount of charcoal and a mass of small bone fragments that were pushed to the back of the firebox as the next meal was being cooked. To the left of the rock line, there was little charcoal, but thirteen pieces of lead casting waste were recovered. These appear to have fallen from the mold onto the dirt fireplace floor, where they were contaminated with dirt and therefore left as waste.

Two musket balls were also recovered from the fireplace area. These measured only 0.57 inches in diameter, noticeably smaller than the ones that were recovered on the Company Street. Musket balls of this smaller diameter were typically used in carbines or pistols. Since an officer's weapon of choice was the pistol, we assume that these were cast for the officer, probably by his servant. One of them was finished, in that the casting channel waste (or sprew) had been clipped off. The other was not. Since it had been found down between two of the fireplace rocks, it appears that it may have been dropped between these rocks when it was hot and thus was deemed not worth the effort and prospective burns to recover.

This unfinished lead ball also had a noticeable ring—one of the reenactors who was a whitesmith for his regiment identified it as the product of an interruption in the casting process such as a sneeze. Such a pause, brief though it may have been, would have been of sufficient duration for the body of the ball to have started to set up and be a different consistency than the rest of the lead when pouring was recommenced. Jim Freebairn, the whitesmith who was also the discoverer of the lead ball, suggested with a broad smile that the servant might have had a cold.[69]

Artifacts that were noticeable by their absence were the remains of clay pipes, at least in the officer's private room. Such ceramic remains, especially clay pipe stems, were ubiquitous in the enlisted men's quarters, testifying to the common habit of smoking and the delicate nature of these types of pipes. There were six small pipe fragments recovered from the east fireplace of the officer's quarters that appear to have been from the same pipe. The absence of such fragments in the private quarters may suggest that Dearborn did not smoke. Such evidence, however, may have also been dutifully cleaned up by his servant, but there seems little question that at least the servant smoked.

Besides these discoveries, there was little else in the artifact record of the officer's hut to serve as clues to his everyday life. There is the evidence of his journal, however, which records the continuous lack of an activity important enough to have been noted, giving the distinct impression of immense boredom. This was probably the result of lack of a well-ordered routine of daily chores such as that which would have occupied the enlisted men. The most frequent entries in Dearborn's journal were "Flanking...," "the old story..." and "nothing new today."[70]

Leisure Time

There was a constant effort to keep enlisted men occupied and out of trouble, and for this reason camp chores were regularly assigned and rotated among them. When they had too much leisure time, it was found that they tended to complain about their problems, both real and imaginary, which led to discontent, loss of morale and, in extreme cases, threats of mutiny and mutiny itself. There was, however, time that the soldier spent that was unoccupied by chores. Their use of this time unfortunately leaves little for the archaeologist to discover and interpret, and only very indirect evidence is available in the historical record. Mention of a ration of one gill of rum will lead to the assumption that time was spent drinking and that drinking was moderate—a gill of rum is a mere quarter of a pint and usually is not enough to lead to inebriation. It is not known, however, whether there were other supplies of liquor available to soldiers through a sutler or other source. There were few courts-martial for drunkenness and disorderly conduct, so we can assume that drinking in the ranks was controlled to a great degree.

Orders frequently hint of other troublesome ways that a soldier could spend his leisure. Card playing, for example, seemed to be a problem because of its attendant gambling, and General Putnam was moved to issue orders in very strong terms against that type of gaming, as well as other types:

> *Discipline must be established and maintained and every person engaged in the Service of his Country ought to devote his whole time and attention to the Duties of his Station: Especially Card playing and gaming of every species is prohibited in the most positive & peremptory terms—No Person of any kind whatever, convicted by a Court Martial of a Violation of this Order must expect and pardon or mitigation of his punishment: and all Officers as they Regard the Interest of the Service & the Honour of their own Corps to see it faithfully carried into execution—all who are possessed of playing Cards are to bring them forth together & make a Burnt Offering of them this evening at Retreat Beating.*[71]

Similarly, for officers there is little information, archaeological or historical, on what they did when not supervising their men. Dearborn, whose journal reflects upper-rank boredom, also contains mention of at least one activity that the officers actively enjoyed when the weather began to moderate in the spring. Under April 3, he recorded: "[A]ll of the Officers of the Brigade turn'd out & Play'd a game at ball the first we have had this year." The type of ballgame that was played is unknown but may have been similar to what later became baseball, with a pitcher, batter and some pattern of bases.

Dearborn's entry clearly reflects the exclusive nature of officer social activity. There was no fraternizing with the rank and file soldiers. This is also clear in Hawkins's description of the camp when he expressed his ignorance of the upper town. This was an area where officers dwelled and thus was off limits to him unless he had express permission to be there. But officers did socialize among themselves, and this may constitute one of the principal ways in which officers occupied their leisure. The social activity of officers can be seen formally in the reconstitution of the Union Lodge of Free Masons, which occurred at Redding in February. This will be treated later in greater detail, but it consisted only of officers and provided a ritual and social outlet for many of them until the next season's campaigns scattered them.

SPECIAL ASSIGNMENTS: A BREAK IN THE ROUTINE

One aspect of life at camp that tended to break up the tedium of the daily routine was the special assignments. The most basic of these was guard duty, sweeping the Company Street, digging and cleaning latrines, but these were really on the order of chores that came to each soldier in rotation. A real break in the camp routine was detached duty, being delegated elsewhere for extended guard duty or for the defense from potential coastal attacks and raids on border farms.

These detached duties grew in number as the winter progressed. The muster rolls show the degree to which this happened and also give some idea of how many men were in camp at different times during the winter. Consider Hawkins's regiment of Canadian Volunteers, for example. In January 1779, 485 men were shown as being enlisted in that regiment. The total number of men fit for duty, however, was 348 after deducting those who were sick in camp or in one of the hospitals. Of those fit for duty, 64 were listed as being on command elsewhere. By March, when Hazen's Canadians left the camp, the total number of men had dropped to 476, with desertions and deaths. Of that number, 303 were fit for duty, and 116 of those were on command elsewhere.[72]

Some of the men delegated to serve elsewhere were "on command" to other departments of the army in the area. For example, several were on guard at the commissary, where they watched over the army's supply depot in Danbury. Others were delegated to help the butcher secure fresh meat for the troops or serve with the blacksmith or with the baker. These men may have had some experience in civilian life in these areas, and their skills were being exploited by the army.

Other men were detached for defensive purposes. On February 4, for example, Dearborn was ordered to march to New London with four hundred men when British troop movements on Long Island were interpreted as a massing for an attack on that city. The men taken from all of the units in all three encampments spent the entire month in New London before it was decided that the attack was not going to materialize and they were ordered back to Redding.

Other detachments were ordered out to patrol the areas of the coast and borderlands abutting Westchester County in New York. The Connecticut coast was subject to frequent British raids for supplies from coastal farms and for the salt from the saltworks that were operating in the coastal shallows of Stamford. Similarly, various lawless elements, known as Cowboys or Skinners, were operating out of Westchester, raiding Connecticut border towns such as Ridgefield and Wilton for cattle and other supplies that they could sell to the British in New York City for scarce hard currency. Several of these patrols were run with the assistance of the local militia and occasionally resulted in fierce fighting. Unfortunately, the accounts of these patrols are rare since there were no regular records kept on them. Often the only mention of them is in pension documents written up to fifty years later—soldiers in the militia used the patrol time to bolster their claims for adequate service time to qualify for the pension. Occasionally, these pension documents give details of skirmishes mentioned nowhere else, but to date no one has mined these sources for sufficient information to piece together a narrative of these defensive activities.

There were still further detachments to join the local coast guard to reinforce coastal defenses. Because of the frequent whale boat raiding from across Long Island Sound by British and Loyalists attempting to raid livestock from the coastal farms, the State of Connecticut set up a series of guard stations and forts along the coast and drafted units of local militia to serve guard duty in them for periods of up to a month. From muster rolls, we know that there were detachments of men from the Redding camps that served on duty with the militia in both Norwalk and Stamford. Fairly regularly, troops were also sent to Horse Neck, now part of Greenwich, to guard border areas against land raids from New York. It was on one of these Horse Neck patrols that General Putnam rode his horse down a steep flight of stairs in an attempt to divert a British patrol. This incident has been commemorated by the statue of his ride by the noted sculptress Anna Hyatt Huntington, about which more will be said later.

As should now be clear, a good general picture of the lifestyle of the average soldier and his commanding officer can be derived from both archaeological and historical sources. Although there are many questions that remain, we have a much richer understanding of what happened at the park than our Victorian predecessors. However, the life in the park consisted of more than daily chores and occasional detached service. There is actually a history of the park for that winter, composed of deeds great and infamous that distinguish the Redding winter camps from the others in Middlebrook and in the Hudson Highlands, and even from those in subsequent years of the war. This history is compiled from the written records and accounts, such as the journals that I have been referencing. Archaeology plays a much smaller part in telling this part of the Redding camp experience, but it was the research that was necessitated by the archaeology that has led to the discovery of new sources that have corrected the history as it was assumed by the park founders.

CHAPTER 4

The History of a Winter Encampment

Although Lieutenant Colonel Henry Dearborn and Sergeant Major John Hawkins recorded little of the mundane activities of camp life in their respective journals, they did a fairly good job of noting the extraordinary events of the winter. We are also fortunate that several orderly books were kept in the Redding camps during that winter, which frequently supplement the information from the journals. Further, oral tradition sometimes supplements the recorded information. Although this evidence must be weighed carefully and skeptically, as in the case of the location of the supposed cemetery on the ridge in back of the monument, it can often contain a kernel of truth that can sometimes lead to the discovery of events that enrich the history.

A good example of oral history embellishing our story is the case of the African American killed by a snowball.[73] According to the oral account, a group of soldiers got into a snowball fight after a heavy snowfall. Among the combatants was an African American, who was often taunted by his white comrades. One of those tormentors packed a ball of snow so tight that it was effectively an ice ball, and he struck the African American in the temple, killing him.

This story, with its vivid details, led us to search the muster rolls looking for an African American in the ranks of the Connecticut, New Hampshire or Canadian soldiers who died during that winter. The search resulted in identifying Zukry Prince of Simsbury, who had enlisted in the Third Connecticut Regiment and who was the only African American who died during that winter. A search of the muster rolls month by month showed that at the beginning of December, he was listed as being sick in Fishkill. He continued to be sick in the Fishkill hospital until his death in February. Obviously, this was not the subject of the story, and the story itself appears to have been more imagination than history, but it did reveal the presence of African Americans in the encampments and it does reflect the type of horseplay among the soldiers that must have broken the boredom of the winter routine. The presence of African Americans has opened up further avenues of research.[74]

ALARMS AND DIVERSIONS

On December 5, just three days after the men had set up their tents and were beginning the task of building huts, the first alarm occurred.[75] According to Dearborn, the alarm went out at midnight that the British were approaching Tarrytown, New York, in an apparent raid on the nearby military supplies. Washington had received intelligence that fifty-two vessels were working their way up the Hudson River, so messengers were sent to all army units within striking distance of the river with orders to mobilize.

The march, consisting of 1,500 men from all three camps, about half the total military population, began about two hours before daylight and proceeded toward Bedford, New York, about twenty miles from Redding. The men arrived that afternoon and deployed themselves to defend the "magazine of provisions" that had been established there. Bedford is about fifteen miles from Tarrytown, and Tarrytown is on the Hudson River and thus vulnerable to attack. The supply depot, therefore, was set up inland, which would force a raiding party to advance overland, giving the local defense forces time to mobilize. The same logic dictated the location of the large regional depot at Danbury, although that did not greatly hinder the British during the deep inland raid of April 1777.

When the British discovered the Redding forces, supplemented by local militia, ready to defend the stores in greater strength than anticipated, they retreated toward Tarrytown, reboarded their vessels and sailed back to New York City. Dearborn's men, not knowing if there would be a renewed attack, spent the night and next day in Bedford. They began their return to camp early on December 8, marching at a leisurely pace to Ridgefield, where they spent the night. The next day, they arrived in camp to renew work on their huts.

Alarms such as this continued throughout the winter. For example, on January 4, Dearborn noted that "we have detached 200 men sent off to Day who were to be Considered an advanced Post to the Division. They are stationed near the Sound." The lesson of the Danbury Raid a year and a half before was still very much in the minds of Fairfield County residents, as well as those who were delegated to protect them. It is not known where along the shore they performed their guard duty, but with two hundred men, they could have been spread among most of the coast guard positions along Long Island Sound, where they would have reinforced the companies of local county militia.

The most notable detachment of this kind occurred on February 4 and had a profound effect on the New Hampshire regiments. In Hawkins's journal under that date, he noted, "This day a very large Detachment...Marched off to New London, in consequence of Genl. Putnam receiving Information from his Excellency Governor Trumbull that an Attack is soon expected from the Enemy on [the] Town of New London and the Shipping in the Harbour. The above Detachment is to guard that Place until the Militia can be called." The reason for the alarm was the movement of a sizable number of British troops to the eastern end of Long Island, along with the movement of other British ships along the sound, giving the appearance of an offensive troop maneuver.

Dearborn's entry of February 2 concerning this detachment is laconic: "I am ordered to take Command of 400 men...& March to New London to garrison that town." The general order for February 3 gives more detail, as it ordered "[t]he Detachment to parade at 10 o'Clock near the Orderly Office with four Days Provisions, Pork and hard Bread, and 30 rounds per Man. The Q. Master will provide four Days Rum which will be carried forward with the Detachment. The Division Q. M. will order two teams to attend the Detachment to transport Officers light Baggage and Camp Kettles."

Dearborn left on February 5, marching as far as Fairfield by the end of the first day. The subsequent stages of his journey are of interest because they show how far a troop of four hundred soldiers could be expected to march daily. By the second day, they got to Milford, the third they camped in New Haven, the fourth in Gilford, the fifth in Killingworth and the sixth in Lime; on the seventh, they ended their march in New London. For a total march of about ninety miles, they averaged twelve to thirteen miles a day. One is left wondering how the four days' provisions they were initially ordered to be in possession of were replenished on a seven-day march.

This duty was far from onerous or boring. Two days after their arrival, Dearborn noted, "[W]e live very happy here." The reason for his pleasure appears in his entry for February 22, in which he noted that "we had an Elligant Ball at which there were a Learge number of very fine Ladies." He further noted no fewer than seven of these balls and two formal dinners over the course of a month and a half. It must have been disappointing when his orders came through to march back to camp on March 20, especially since the expected attack never materialized.

THE MUTINY

In the early days of the Redding camps, there was a harbinger of things to come, even though it did not directly affect the New Hampshire or Canadian regiments. On December 28, Dearborn noted that "there is general uneaseyness among soldiers of Genrl Putnam's Division on account of the Depresiation of our Currency the Consequences of which I fear will Prove unhappy." This uneasiness was most acute among the Connecticut men in Huntington's brigade, camped in West Redding. Unlike the New Hampshire troops, who were relatively well supplied and paid by their state, the Connecticut regiments had not been as well served by their government in Hartford. They did not share immediately in the French largesse with regard to clothing, they had not been paid in several months and when they had been paid, it was in rapidly depreciating paper money issued by the state. In fact, 1779 was a year of the most precipitous depreciation, during which the Continental dollar decreased in value by 229 percent.[76]

Two days after Dearborn's journal entry, a spark was struck that threatened to blow into a full conflagration. A day of Thanksgiving, Dearborn noted, "This is Thanksgiving Day through out the Continent our men have Half a Pint of Rum Each to keep it with." The rum, it appears, lubricated the tensions, making them more volatile.

Late in the morning of December 30, a large contingent of troops fell into line on the parade ground, fully armed and ready to advance on Hartford for redress of their grievances, at the point of a bayonet if necessary. They had been stirred up by their sergeants to the point that they openly disobeyed the orders of the company officers to return to their quarters. At his headquarters on Umpewaug Road, Putnam was quickly notified and just as quickly galloped off for the Huntington camp.

What came next is reported by David Humphreys, who at the time was Putnam's aide-de-camp and an eyewitness to these events. Approaching the troops, Putnam was shown every respect due a commanding officer. He demanded to know under whose orders the troops were assembled. In reply, he got a full list of grievances, including deficiencies in clothing and blankets, as well as being "paid" in worthless currency that hadn't even been given to them in many months; ultimately, they were exasperated by the promises that had been made by the state and not kept. In response, Putnam's tone was sympathetic, earnest and rather stirring:

> *My brave lads, whither are you going? Do you intend to desert your officers, and to invite the enemy to follow you into the country? Whose cause have you been fighting and suffering so long in—is it not your own? Have you no property, no parents, wives or children? You have behaved like men so far—all of the world is full of your praises—and posterity will stand astonished at your deeds: but not if you spoil all at last. Don't you consider how much the country is distressed by the war, and your officers have not been any better paid than yourselves? But we all expect better times, and that the country will do us ample justice. Let us all stand by one another, then, and fight it out like brave soldiers. Think what a shame it would be for Connecticut men to run away from their officers.*[77]

The original source for this speech is David Humphreys, who wrote and published the first biography of Putnam several years after the war, but even though it is undoubtedly not verbatim, it probably follows closely the sentiment that Putnam expressed that day. The speech had the desired effect. Upon concluding, Putnam turned to the brigade major and directed him to march the men to their respective parade areas and have them stack their arms. The men shouldered their firearms and marched back to their quarters. The potential mutiny was defused.

As for the ringleader, Grumman's account of the mutiny goes on to repeat some folklore that has endured to the present. The principal ringleader was not let off as easily as the men he instigated. This offending sergeant was ordered to be held in the guardhouse, but after a short time he tried to escape and was shot dead by a sentry on duty who himself had been one of the potential mutineers. Up until a few years ago, the sign on the replicated guardhouse in the park told the same story to the delight of youngsters, who were fascinated by the fact that a man had died right there.

The truth is a little more prosaic but important to understanding some of Putnam's later actions. In an order dated January 20, he responded to a petition of several officers who pleaded for clemency for the six sergeants and one corporal who had been identified as the ones responsible for precipitating the disorderly behavior. Claiming that they were responding to the heat of the moment and acknowledging their greater value in the fighting ranks, he sent them back to their respective regiments with the stern warning that any further such behavior would be met with "Vindictive Justice…Without possible mitigation."[78]

These orders, nor any other records, including our two journal keepers, do not make any mention of an escaping prisoner being shot to death. The orders do make clear that seven ringleaders were identified, not one, and that they were ultimately treated with leniency after a period of incarceration lasting twenty-one days. It would be pleasant to note that Putnam's speech had a lasting effect, but it should be noted that a full-force mutiny the next winter at Morristown was again initiated by the Connecticut regiments.[79] A more immediate consequence of Putnam's leniency, however, was the gradual breakdown of camp discipline, which led to the tragic February executions.

The effect of the discontent among the Connecticut troops had only an indirect effect on the New Hampshire and Canadian troops in the east camp. Colonel Hazen responded to the events of December 30 in a general order read before his troops the next day.[80] In his peculiarly preachy way, he commended his troops for not being tempted to follow the ill-advised lead of their Connecticut brethren. He then went on for several pages of the orderly book to comment on how awful it was to lack loyalty and discipline. Meanwhile, Dearborn did not mention the aborted mutiny at all after noting his warning that there was discontent in the ranks. (Hawkins's entries for the days surrounding the mutiny are regrettably missing from his journal.)

Crime, Punishment and Executions

Any army at any time has a constant problem of maintaining discipline in its ranks. This is especially true during winter encampments, when troops are relatively idle once they have completed their camp routines. On a weekly basis, courts-martial were held, and the accounts of them in the orderly books for this winter are a catalogue of crimes both petty and serious, as well as a list of punishments extending from mild exhortation to execution.

The easiest and most frequently used tool for maintaining order in camp was the general order. As noted above, when gambling and the use of cards were seen as problems, there was an order banning cards from the camp and prohibiting games of chance, whatever they might have been. This gave the officers in the field authorization to stop such behavior with a court-martial and corporal punishment if necessary. Another problem was perceived to be practice drumming among the camp's drum corps. Because drums were used to signal events, the random drumming of one of the musicians either for practice or recreation could not be tolerated. In the general orders for May 9, then, drum practice was relegated to being held from four to five o'clock in the morning or from six to seven o'clock in the evening: "Any Drummer who is found Practicing at any other than the time Mentioned Shall be Severely Punished."[81] There is no indication what that punishment would have been, but it must have been mild, probably no more than a reprimand. Since this order was issued in the final days of the center and west encampments, the disruption of drumming could not have been a serious problem or it would have merited attention earlier in the season.

Wasting powder, on the other hand, was considered serious. Gunpowder was an important resource for an eighteenth-century army, and wasting it could have serious repercussions in future engagements with the enemy. The orders of February 24 noted that "the Commander is sorry to find an unnecessary waist of Ammunition in the Brigades, he positively forbids any man blasting of Logs or fencing in ye Neighborhood of Camp."[82] The next day, there was an alarm, and a detachment from the Connecticut regiments was issued ammunition and marched to "the Crossroads leading to Wilton." As so often happened, the alarm came to nothing, and the troops were marched back into camp later that day. The next morning, the brigade orders were careful to note that the ammunition that had been issued was to be returned to the quartermaster of each regiment, "who will take Proper care of it," and thus curb recreational musket firing.

Precautions such as this did not appear to have much effect, and ammunition continued to go missing. In the brigade orders of May 22, General Putnam noticed "with surprise the great waste of Ammunition, no less than five thousand cartridges that are not accounted for by Yesterday's returns since last Monthly Returns."[83] Accordingly, he ordered every officer of the companies to examine the men's cartridge boxes every evening at roll call, obliging them to account for all cartridges given to them. Any cartridges not accounted for or "wantonly wasted" were to be paid for by dunning the pay of the soldiers who were responsible for them. Knowing how poorly and irregularly the troops were paid, one wonders how effective this punishment was.

The unaccounted-for gunpowder quite probably was used for hunting and foraging to supplement the meager diet. This may account for the wild animal species tentatively identified by David Poirier in his 1970s excavations and for the appearance of poultry bones that we recovered. It was also a factor in a rebellious incident that was reported by Joseph Martin in the center encampment.

At about the same time that the troops of Huntington's brigade in West Redding were being cajoled by Putnam for their incipient mutiny, there were rumblings of mutiny in the center encampment. The men turned out on the parade ground, but not under arms, and the officers were able to get them back into their quarters without serious trouble, but the thwarted soldiers came up with another way to make their discontent known. Although they were restive and watched by the officers, some of the soldiers managed to get an old gun barrel, which they then set up in an unfinished hut. Loading it to about one-third full, they attached a slow match that would allow them time to sneak back to their own quarters before it set the charge off with a resounding roar. This roused the officers, who ran about scolding the rank and file as they tried unsuccessfully to find who had committed the crime of firing in camp. No one, it seemed, knew who had made the noise nor where it had come from. In Plumb's words, "This farce was carried on the greater part of the night; but at length the officers getting tired of running so often to catch Mr. Nobody, without finding him, that they soon gave up the chase, and the men seeing that they could no longer gull the officers, gave up the business likewise."[84]

Most courts-martial dealt with more serious maters. For example, as part of a series of trials for February 4 through February 6, Asa Thayer of the 8th Connecticut was found guilty of breaking open the quartermaster store at Danbury and stealing a number of shoes. For this theft, he was sentenced to receive one hundred lashes on his naked back, to be administered the next morning at "Troop Beating" (the drum call for morning muster). The application of lashes "well laid on" was the most common corporal punishment, and when the number reached levels as that for Thayer, it would be done in stages and leave the man half dead.[85]

A lesser crime was Lamson Mallery's (of the 6th Connecticut), who was found guilty of stealing a horse and selling it. He was sentenced to sixty lashes on the naked back. Isaac Moore of Walker's Artillery Company was found guilty of stealing $300 from Lieutenant Hitchcock of Bethel. This was considered as serious a crime as stealing shoes, and Moore was sentenced to one hundred lashes and then was expected to refund the $300 to Hitchcock by "regular stoppage of his Wages, provide, as it appears, there was others concerned in the taking of said money who if properly convicted of the same ought to bear their equal Proportions of the Sum to be refunded." Nowhere, however, does it indicate that these other miscreants were to share the lashes.

Among the most serious crimes tried by these courts-martial was desertion. Sergeant Ebenezer Byington of the 6th Connecticut was found guilty of that crime and was sentenced to receive one hundred lashes on the bare back; then he was returned to the ranks after paying the sergeant who apprehended him the expenses he had incurred. Earlier, Benjamin Nobles of the 5th Connecticut was found guilty of desertion and going over to the enemy, as well as persuading others to go over to the enemy as well. For this he was also sentenced to one hundred lashes. The court apparently made no distinction as to whether the deserter was simply guilty of walking away from camp or actually going to serve the enemy.

One desertion case is worthy of special attention because it was one of the few that occurred in Colonel Hazen's Canadian regiment and had ramifications for further attempts to maintain discipline. On January 11, a court-martial was convened for which Lieutenant Colonel Henry Dearborn was president. The court found that William Brown and George Pitcher, both soldiers in Hazen's regiment, were guilty of desertion, and they were sentenced to one hundred lashes, as well as being forced to reimburse thirty dollars to the inhabitants who were responsible for capturing them and marching them back to camp. As was usual for all army court cases, the sentence was referred to the commanding officer, in this case Hazen, for his approval. In all but a few rare cases, this approval was given and the sentence quickly carried out. This was one of those rare cases. He approved of the sentences but noted in his usual preachy fashion: "[H]e is induced to believe that those unfortunate Prisoners have been deluded and inticed away from their Duty and Allegiance to the United States by wicked and ill-minded people in this neighborhood, he is pleased to remit the Corporal Punishment, and takes this public Opportunity to warn them and others against like Criminal Conduct; the Infamy which justly follows Perjury, the Disgrace if the Whipping Post, or Halter on the Gallows are Punishments generally annexed to the approbious Crime of Desertion." The moralizing then goes on for another page of the orderly book before he is through.

Moses Hazen was well meaning but naïve. The leniency that he showed did nothing to curb the rate of desertion, which as the winter proceeded became one of Commander Putnam's biggest problems. Only somewhat more serious was the incidence of spies who seemed to penetrate the porous defenses of the camps with ease, obtaining intelligence on troop strength and condition that they transmitted back to the British in New York. Both of these crimes became so chronic that in late January Putnam put forth his intention to deal harshly with the next cases that were brought to him.

He did not have to wait long. On February 4, Edward Jones was found guilty of "going to the enemy as a guide and coming out as a spy." During the trial, it came out that Jones was born in Wales and was accordingly loyal to the king. At the time that hostilities broke out, he was living in Ridgefield but fled to the British for protection after they took New York. There he became a butcher and had been sent into Westchester County to purchase cattle for the king's forces when he had been apprehended after mistakenly crossing over the line into Connecticut. The court, pressured by Putnam's desire to return discipline to the ranks, was not inclined to believe that he had innocently wandered into the state, especially in the area around Ridgefield that he knew well, and he was sentenced to death. Putnam obviously approved the sentence and "ordered it to be put into Execution on Friday the 12th instant between the hours of 10 & 12 o'clock by hanging him by the neck until he is Dead, Dead, Dead." From the orders, it is clear that there was to be no question of his physical state after the sentence was carried out.

Two days later, there was another court-martial and another serious crime for which death was the usual punishment. John Smith had been a soldier in the 1st Connecticut Regiment but apparently had an epiphany during which he experienced the revelation that the true cause was with the British. He deserted, only to be apprehended on his way to the British lines and returned to camp. His court-martial clearly found him guilty; in reaction to this, he persisted in saying that he would again go over to the enemy if he ever had a chance. His statements further ensured his fate, and Putnam approved the sentence of being shot to death.

Now that he had two prisoners under sentence of death, Putnam decided to deal with them both at the same time and set the date of their demise as February 16. Meanwhile, they were to be kept at the guardhouse on Umpawaug Road. While there, they were subject to harassment. The soldiers of all three camps were commanded to be in attendance, but these were to be public executions, so the civilian population was also expected to witness this most gruesome spectacle in Redding's history. The prisoners' presence in the guardhouse was too enticing for both the public's and soldiers' moral sensibilities, so they showed up with some frequency to taunt the condemned. This led Putnam to issue orders on February 13 that no persons were to be allowed access to the prisoners, "as frequent Complaints have been made that they are interrupted in their private Devotions by People who come for not other Reason than to insult them."[86]

As the fateful day approached, there was some sympathy for the condemned. Reverend Bartlett, the minister of the Redding Congregational Church, approached Putnam to ask for at least a stay of execution for Smith until the case could be reviewed by Washington. Putnam was not to be moved, and the orders went out the next day that the prisoners were to be conducted to the Redding meetinghouse, where a sermon regarding them was to be preached, ironically by Reverend Bartlett. On the fifteenth, orders were issued that the brigades "were to parade to Morrow morning a 9 o'clock well dress'd and equip'd to attend the Execution of the prisoners under the Sentence of Death." The presence of the troops, especially the men with whom the condemned had served, was standard military procedure and was necessary so the punishment could serve as a moral lesson on the consequences of spying and desertion. This is an important point to keep in mind when considering the events of the sixteenth.

The place of execution is still remembered as Gallows Hill. The precise location was on a terrace just east of the triangle made by the intersection of the west portion of Gallows Hill Road with Whortleberry Road. The land to the west of this terrace forms an immense natural amphitheater, which would have allowed the combined crowd of soldiers from all three of the camps, as well as a large number of spectators, to get a clear view of the executions. Visitors to this site today must remember that the eighteenth-century hillside was denuded of all trees, yielding clear sightlines that are difficult to imagine with the second-growth forest that now luxuriates on the side of the hill.

The events of that fatal day are most accurately given by Hawkins, who was an eyewitness and who wrote about the event later that same day (no account appears in Dearborn's journal since he was in New London at the time):

Gallows Hill as it appeared in 1905. The terrace just below the crest of the hill is where the executions took place. Denuded of the trees seen here, it would have allowed three thousand soldiers to witness the punishment with unobstructed views.

> *February 16th—This Day Edward Jones was hanged and John Smith was shot, about three Miles from our Camp, in the Presence of Genls. Parson's. Poor's and Huntington's Brigades, who appeared under Arms and a vast concourse of Country People from far and near attended...Before Jones was hanged, the Revd. Dr. Evans, Chaplain of our Brigade, made a long Discourse well adapted to the occasion. Jones went out of this world not seeming much concerned, but Smith seemed greatly affected; he was extremely weak and fainting when he was lead* [sic] *by Dr. Evans from the Gallows to the Place were* [sic] *he was to be shot, which was at least two Hundred Yards.*

Other details of the executions are given in the oral traditions that have survived. Although these are less reliable, the shocking nature of the events of that day etched them deeply in public memory and may give some added understanding of the proceedings.[87]

Grumman described the gallows as being twenty feet in height, with a ladder leading up to the noose. According to his account, Jones mounted the ladder, but the man responsible for overturning it to perform the actual execution was mysteriously not present, and so Putnam ordered him to jump. Logically, Jones refused to effectively commit suicide, and someone else had to be recruited to do the fatal deed. There is another eyewitness account of the hanging that clarifies the sequence of events recollected many years later in the pension application of James Sanford: "I will recollect that when Jones mounted the ladder, he protested his innocence, to which General Putnam replied that he would hear none of his jaw, and ordered the ladder to be turned over."[88]

John Warner Barber, when writing about the hanging in 1836, recounted that in the absence of the delegated hangman, two twelve-year-old boys were pressed into duty. Sobbing and crying, they were ordered forward, and when they asked to be excused, Putnam compelled them to become executioners with his drawn sword. Barber then drew some unwarranted conclusions about Putnam's cruel personality.[89] This story appears nowhere else in the literature of that winter, and from all of the other evidence on Putnam's personality, it is safe to ignore this as a piece of gossip that was probably given to Barber by someone who personally disliked Putnam (quite likely a local Loyalist).

The account of Smith and his firing squad that Hawkins gave in such a cursory fashion can also be fleshed out by Grumman's account. Hawkins clearly claimed that the execution of Smith took place about two hundred yards (the distance of about two modern football fields) from the gallows. Given the topography of this part of Gallows Hill, that would have to be in a northerly direction along Whortleberry Road. Smith was half dragged to this spot, where a small firing squad was assembled. There, according to Grumman, he was subjected to a volley at near point-blank range—so close, in fact, that his clothing caught fire. The three musket balls that penetrated his breast caused him to fall forward onto his face, but his convulsing body flopped over onto its back. Since he was apparently still alive, the officer in command of the firing squad had to come forward and finish the job with a musket ball to the brain. The lifeless body was then placed into a coffin, and with his clothes still smoldering, every soldier in the three encampments was forced to march by and view the remains, while a sergeant stationed at the head of the coffin watched to make sure that each soldier looked at the remains. In this way, Smith's death served as an unusually poignant reminder of what awaited any man who deserted.

Although the account of the firing squad sounds unnaturally gruesome, it follows the normal military procedures for such executions. The duty officer, usually a sergeant, was responsible for determining that the firing squad had done its job and for administering a fatal shot to the head if it had not. Likewise, the same officer was responsible for making sure that every soldier, and especially those in the offender's company, saw the mangled remains as an object lesson. The account is grisly, but in comparison to other such accounts, it rings true. These executions also appear to have accomplished their purpose in that the incidence of courts-martial diminished, especially for the serious crimes of spying and desertion.

An interesting footnote to the executions appeared in the Redding column of the *Newtown Bee* in its October 23, 1891 issue. Judge Pickett had visited the park the week before and told the park staff that he had visited the old campground fifty years before, when he was twelve years old. In the process, his father took him to the various sites associated with the Redding camps, including the execution site on Gallows Hill. Even though he had not been there in half a century, he claimed that he could show them the place where "those two British spies were buried at the foot of the gibbet." According to the article, "He did so and even found an old and marked stone that had become sunken down into the ground and nearly obscured. He righted the stone and identified the inscription."[90]

There is a ring of authenticity to the story in that it has long been a custom in both military and civilian executions to bury the victim's body at the base of the instrument of his death. Therefore, it is distinctly possible that the remains of Jones and Smith lay at the Gallows Hill Road intersection. There is no independent documentation for this, however, nor have the remains or the marked stone ever been systematically searched for. Such a search remains to be a project of some future archaeological investigation using remote sensing devices such as ground-penetrating radar or maybe just a crude probe to locate the now reburied stone marker.

PUTNAM'S HEROIC RIDE

Another incident that has become part of the folklore and history of Putnam Park is General Putnam's heroic ride down the outdoor staircase in Horse Neck. Horse Neck is today part of Greenwich, and being on the border with Westchester County, it was a critical spot for skirmishes between British forces and defending Patriots. For most of the winter, this had been a place of detached coastal guard duty for soldiers from the camps. Not only were they there to protect the farmers from depredations of the lawless elements foraging for livestock and other supplies that could be profitably sold to the British, but they also guarded the salt pans along the southwest Connecticut coast—places where seawater was evaporated to produce scarce salt for the army.

This section of Greenwich was split into two areas by a ledge of bedrock. In the upper section was a meetinghouse in front of which Putnam had stationed a small force of about 150 men with two old iron cannons, creating a commanding defensive position. The lower section was where the main body of citizens lived, and to facilitate their climb up the steep hill to the meetinghouse, a flight of seventy stairs had been sculpted into the face of the ledge rock.

On February 26, Putnam was on a visit of inspection and had stayed overnight in a small cottage in the upper section. That morning, a scout warned Putnam during his morning grooming of the approach of General Tryon with a body of 1,500 troops, a force about three-fourths the size he had with him on the raid on Danbury in the spring of 1777. As these troops came into view, he quickly realized that they so heavily outnumbered his small force that an offensive thrust was impossible. Tryon's men changed formation to allow the troops with horses to charge, and Putnam ordered the cannons discharged and his men to disperse into the swamp behind them, where horses and troops would have difficulty following. He, on the other hand, rode through the cannon smoke toward Tryon, and once engaging the attention of the troopers, he veered toward the stairs.

Accounts differ regarding what happened next. According to David Humphreys, Putnam dashed toward the precipice and then plunged down the stairs as the British troopers were just a sword stroke behind him.[91] Looking at the severe drop, they held back, realizing that their horsemanship was not up to the steepness of the stairs. Using their carbines, they tried to shoot him, but he rode safely to the base of the stairs, with only his hat shot off his head. By the time the troopers had ridden around to the base of the hill, Putnam had made good his escape, riding hard toward Stamford.

Once in Stamford, he regrouped the forces that had been with him in the upper part of the town and supplemented them with local militia. With this force, he harassed Tryon's retreat, managing to capture fifty prisoners in the process. According to this account, Putnam approached the British lines the next day and exchanged the prisoners he had taken. To compensate Putnam for the loss of his hat, and for the respectful treatment he had given to the British prisoners, Tryon sent him a suit of clothes—or, as another account claims, just a new hat to replace the one shot from his head.

Recently, another description of this famous ride was uncovered in the pension files of Joseph Rundel.[92] Rundel was originally from New Fairfield and was sixteen years old when he enlisted in one of the Connecticut regiments about two days before the incident in Horse Neck. He was part of the force guarding that section of coast when Putnam noticed him. Telling him that he was too young to be part of the Connecticut line, he offered to take him on as his waiter or orderly. He was serving in this position when Tryon's troops approached. Then, in his own words:

> *Our men had stationed near the meetinghouse a cannon or two, which fired upon the enemy until they approached in so great a force and so near, that General Putnam ordered his men to retreat and save themselves as best they could. He also retreated on his horse at full speed, pursued closely by the British horse. He made down a flight of stone steps, the top of which were about 60 yards (I should think) from the meetinghouse. He did not ride down more than fifteen or twenty of them (there being, I think about one hundred of them in the whole) Then he dismounted and led the horse as fast as possible. I was at the bottom of the steps as soon as he was. He then mounted his horse, told me to make my escape to a swamp not far off, and he rode off.*

Rundel did not make good his escape and was captured by one of the British troopers after tripping while trying to get to the swamp. He was taken to the Sugar House, a notorious prison in New York, where he was allowed a good deal of freedom due to his youth and small size. He eventually took advantage of this to escape and make his way back to Putnam, whom he served as a waiter for another five weeks or so, until the camp broke up. His account differs in detail but not in its emphasis on the heroic qualities of Putnam and the concern that he had for his men.

Meanwhile, back in Redding, Hawkins had heard about the Horse Neck fray that same day, but with few details: "At 4 o'Clock in the Afternoon News arrived at our Camp, from our Men at Horse Neck, giving an Account of the Enemy's Approach there, & of a Skirmish that happened; the Particulars of which I have not yet received any account that I can give full Credit to." The reaction to this news in camp was predictably military in its indecision. The brigade was immediately under arms, but after a short interval they were dismissed. Two hours later, six artillery pieces from two of the brigades were discharged, and the troops again turned out ready for action, but since the signal had not been completed as properly set down in the brigade orders, the men were ordered to stand down and return to their huts until further orders. Those orders came very shortly after the order to stand down, and the men appeared under arms and properly equipped. This time they marched off. It was just at daybreak when they joined the men from the two Connecticut brigades and marched south to Horse Neck. They only went about six miles when they were ordered to return to camp, which they did without knowing what the fuss had been about, although details continued to filter back up to Hawkins over the next few days.

Because of Putnam's heroics and humanitarian nature, and since this now famous ride occurred during the period of the Redding camps, the noted sculptress Anna Hyatt Huntington chose to use that subject for her last epic equestrian statue. She produced this when she was in her mid-nineties, pulling herself up and down the larger-than-life clay model in a bosun's chair. Once cast in bronze, it was given to the state to be exhibited at the park, and it has now been moved into a prominent position in front of the pavilion/visitors' center.

THE AMERICAN UNION LODGE NO. 1: THE MILITARY MASONS IN REDDING

One of the major social diversions of the Redding encampment was the re-formation of the American Union Lodge of Free Masons. This fraternal order was restricted to the commissioned officers in Redding, and since its minute book has survived, we have an unusually clear glimpse into high-ranking social life.

This lodge had its origins on February 13, 1776, in Roxbury, Massachusetts, shortly before the American siege of Boston was ended due to the evacuation of the British forces. This lodge was unusual in that it did not have a permanent location as do most Masonic lodges. Because the members were constantly moving around, they formed a mobile lodge, or military lodge, as it was formally known later. The lodge lapsed in August 1776, disrupted by the loss of the Battle of Long Island and the dispersal of the principal members to locations far from one another.

After the Connecticut troops were safely in their winter quarters in Redding, however, General Samuel Parsons went about re-forming lodge. He had been a founding member at its first formation and served as its first treasurer, so it was logical that he was the motivating force behind its re-formation. A formal call for the reassembly of the lodge was sent out on February 10, 1778, and on the fifteenth, the first meeting of the reconstituted lodge was held at the house of Widow Sanford, near the old meetinghouse. From this description, the location of Widow Sanford's was near the Redding town green, which was just in front of the present Congregational Church and Town House, since the old meetinghouse was located on the western end of that green. (The new meetinghouse was built on the north end of Great Pasture Road in 1753.)

Subsequent to February 15, the Masons had a busy schedule, meeting a total of seventeen times between then and May 7, when the Connecticut troops finally began to leave the camps for the spring campaigns. In addition to their regular meetings, they had at least two elaborate dinners or "Feasts" that were held on March 25 and April 7. These are of interest historically because they list most of the officers who were members, as well as several citizens of the civilian population who had also become members and who would be responsible for forming a Redding Masonic lodge after the army vacated the camps. They are also significant because the details recorded by the Masonic secretary give an unprecedented glimpse into the upper-crust social life of the time. It is worth including here the secretary's account of the first feast since it is such an important part of the history of the winter encampment.

On March 22, it was voted that an Entered Apprentice Lodge be held on Thursday, March 25, at 2:00 p.m. "and that Bros. Belding, Sill, and Little prepare a dinner and invite the Brethren of the ancient society, who are not members of this Lodge, to dine with us. That Bro. Redfield wait on the Hon. Bro. Putnam with the desire of the Lodge to attend; that Mrs. Sanford, her daughter and niece, Mrs. Marshall and Heart, be also invited to dine with us on Thursday."

The lodge was opened at the advertised hour with eleven members present. Three men were accepted by individual ballots, and they were duly made Entered Apprentices. The lodge was then closed at 4:30 p.m., and a procession was formed that marched the whole company a short distance to Widow Sanford's house, where the feast would be held.[93] The order of this procession was:

1. *Bro. Whitney to clear the way.*
2. *The Wardens with their wands*
3. *The youngest Brother with the Bag*
4. *Brethren by Juniority*
5. *The Worshipful Master, with the Treasurer on his right hand, supporting the Sword of Justice and the Secretary on his left hand, supporting the Bible, Square, and Compasses*
6. *Music, playing the Entered Apprentice March advanced twenty yards in front, and proceeded to Esq. Hawleys where Bro. Little delivered a few sentiments on Friendship, and Rev. Dr. Evans and a number of gentlemen and Ladies being present.*

After dinner, the following songs and toasts were given, interspersed with music, for the entertainment of the company:

Song: Hail America; Toast: General Washington; Music: Grand March.
Song: Montgomery; Toast: in Memory of Warren, Montgomery, Wooster; Music: Dead March.
Song: French Ladies Lament; Toast: Relief of the Widows and Orphans; Music: Country Jig.
Song: Mason's Daughter; Toast: Ladies of America; Music: Mason's Daughter.
Song: On, on, my Dear Brethren; Toast: Union Harmony & Peace
Song: Huntsmen; Toast: Social Enjoyment.
Song: My Dog and Gun; Toast: Contentment.

The festivities were concluded with a speech by Brother Waldo. At half past seven o'clock, the procession began returning to the lodge room, in reverse order from the afternoon procession, with the music playing "The Mason's Daughter."

The master having taken his seat, the lodge opened, after which Worshipful Brother Heart returned his thanks to the officers and brethren for their faithful attendance in labor and in transacting the business of the day with the greatest decorum and harmony. The lodge gave expression in formal order, as follows:

> *Voted That the Lodge have a grateful sense of the honor paid them by the Rev. Dr. Evans and other gentlemen and ladies in attending the exercises of the day.*
>
> *Voted That the thanks of the Lodge be presented to Bros, Little and Waldo for the honor conferred on the Lodge by their addresses.*[94]

In addition to the sense of what eighteenth-century formal dinners were like, this account is significant because it documents the presence of Abigence Waldo in Redding. He was a surgeon and therefore held officer rank. He also appears to have been a well-regarded Mason since he addressed the assembled Masons during this as well as the second feast on April 7. The topic of his speeches are unknown but were undoubtedly on the nature of Masonic history and practice.

During the Redding encampments, he was part of the 1st Regiment of Connecticut line, which was camped under Huntington's command in the westernmost encampment. He had joined the regiment with the re-formation of the Continental army in January 1, 1777, and had served until October 1, 1779, when he resigned due to ill health. He is most well known for the journal he kept the previous winter at Valley Forge, which has given scholars one of the best descriptions of the difficult conditions at that notorious encampment. Unfortunately, his journal entries for the Redding winter have not been located, if they ever existed, but his extant accounts make him one of the most important Revolutionary personalities in Redding that winter.

The Masonic feast on March 25 was held on the day that the Canadian volunteers under General Hazen began to leave camp. They had completely left by March 30, so the Putnam Park encampment became somewhat subdued. As early as the twenty-sixth, Dearborn had returned with the last of the men who had been sent for detached duty in New London, and immediately upon their return, they began preparations for the departure of all three New Hampshire regiments for the Hudson Highlands. By mid-April, they had left the camp, leaving it almost deserted. The Connecticut encampments would not leave for almost another month, but the town of Redding was beginning to settle back into an almost normal routine. As the deserted huts fell into disrepair, many of the present features of the encampment developed. Because of this, the departure from the camps and their deconstruction is an important part of the creation of what is today known as Putnam Memorial State Park.

CHAPTER 5

The Troops March Out

THE FATE OF A WINTER ENCAMPMENT

It had only been three and a half months since Sergeant Major John Hawkins had wearily trudged into the wooded valley that would briefly be his home. It was now approaching spring. The weather had not modified completely; there was a very heavy snowstorm on March 24, but temperatures were beginning to moderate. The first rumblings of the rumor mill were being heard indicating that there were special plans being laid for the Canadians in the coming few months. Anticipation began to replace the gloom of winter.

Orders preparing for marching out have not survived. This was partially due to the small number of men involved in this first troop movement. The muster rolls indicate that only 313 men were on or fit for duty in March, 245 of whom were rank and file soldiers.[95] Since these men constituted a single regiment, only one orderly book was kept, by John Jones, recording the sequence of preparatory orders. Regrettably, the entries in Jones's book effectively stop in February, and another orderly book with subsequent entries has not been found.

The first indication that Hazen's men were beginning to stir was Hawkins's entry for March 13 in which he recorded, "Yesterday and today the most of our different Commands have returned to Camp; they were sent for in Consequence of our Regiment being on the move." Nine days later, he noted, "The remainder of our Commands Have returned and joined," and in the entry for the next day the nature of the mission becomes a little clearer, including a note on the way the march out of camp was to proceed: "This day our Regt. received orders to march to Springfield, in the Massachusetts Bay being ordered on a particular separate service. For the more Conveniencey of marching and lodging at Nights, the Regt. is divided into three Divisions; the first Division is ordered to march tomorrow."

It seems that the order to march on March 24 was a bit premature. Six companies of the regiment, constituting the first division, were to be ready to march but were prevented by a snowstorm that was characterized by Hawkins as "the deepest snow that we have had here this winter." The division finally set off the next day, and the following day (March 26), at 6:00 a.m., the six companies of the second division followed the first. The third division then moved out at 6:00 p.m. on the same day, but the baggage wagons carrying the possessions of the soldiers and the officers that could not be carried on their backs milled about in confusion, delaying the departure of Hazen's final contingent.

Hawkins himself was delayed yet further and did not leave until March 30, when he left with Colonel Hazen and a number of other officers, forming a rear guard to escort the colonel's baggage. The last entry in his journal for the Redding encampment gives some idea of the conditions under which they began their march: "At Dark we arrived in Newtown. The Roads was very wet and Dirty owing to the last great Snow melting away."

The destination of Springfield, Massachusetts, was part of a ruse to hide the actual nature of the project that Washington had quietly agreed to at Hazen's urging. The colonel had extensive landholdings in Canada south of the St. Lawrence River, below Montreal. It was from the primarily French population of this area that he had recruited most of his regiment. The animosity between the French and their English conquerors was such that the American commanders, including Hazen, held out great hope that with a little provocation they could be induced to rise up and join the American cause. Even though this had not occurred four years before during the initial ill-fated invasion of Quebec, hope still remained that this discontented faction of the Canadian population could be mobilized to American advantage. For this second invasion and uprising to be successful, however, a road was needed to get troops and supplies to southern Canada through the wilderness of Vermont, hopefully with some degree of stealth. It was to be the task of Hazen's men to accomplish that goal during the summer of 1779.[96]

By May, the regiment had stopped at Springfield long enough to gather supplies and then pushed on northward to the small settlement of Wells River. Beginning here in 1776, General Bayley had been surveying the path of the road to the northwest, but with the collapse of the first invasion the survey had been shelved. With the revival of the plan, Hazen immediately went to work on Bayley's survey, and by August, he had pushed through the uncompleted road as far as a mountain pass that to this day bears his name:

Hazen's Notch. The road was never completed to Canada nor was it used for the intended invasion since the center of war activity moved toward the southern states, and efforts to complete the road to and beyond the Canadian border stalled.

After the Revolution, the Bayley-Hazen Road facilitated the creation of settlements in the interior of Vermont. For a while in the early years of the nineteenth century, there was an attempt to use this road as the basis of a turnpike to Canada, but it was not very successful and the project was aborted. Today, the road still exists in part as local roads in the towns through which it passes, but it is only remembered by the historic markers at its beginning in Wells River and at the terminus in Hazen's Notch.

Meanwhile, Back in Redding

Lieutenant Colonel Henry Dearborn, upon his return from New London, found himself in a command vacuum. Although General Enoch Poor was the ranking officer in the eastern encampment, and the brigade camped there was known as Poor's brigade, Poor had been on furlough since the beginning of the winter, as had most of the officers ranking immediately below him. This left Colonel Hazen as the ranking officer in Redding, and command of the New Hampshire and Canadian troops fell to him. Accordingly, he billeted himself just to the south of the camp in a wing of Colonel John Read's homestead, Lonetown Manor.

This building no longer stands at the corner of Route 107 (Putnam Park Road) and Lonetown Road, but sections of the foundation of the building have recently been found there by Stewart Reeve.[97] The Lonetown farm built by John Read Sr. in about 1711 was one of the first houses built in the area that would become Redding. The farm included more than five hundred acres and extended from the Bethel border down to Cross Highway. The present area of Putnam Park was located within the northern portion of this farm, which would have important consequences as camps depopulated in late spring. It was logical, therefore, that the commanding officer at the park would find lodging at the manor house now in the hands of Read's son, Colonel John Read Jr.[98]

Upon his arrival back in camp, Dearborn was greeted by the news that the whole brigade was under marching orders and that Hazen's regiment had begun to march out of camp. That same day, he also noted that a detachment of one hundred New Hampshire troops had marched to Peekskill, but it is not clear why they left before the rest of the brigade. March

30 found Dearborn in an unusual situation. He noted, "I take command of the Brigade." And the next day, he noted, "I take Quarters at Colo. Read's where Col. Hazen has Quartered…A very agreeable family." It is at this point that he abandoned the large officer's hut that we excavated on top of the ridge, where the cemetery was purported to be.

Dearborn's ascendancy to command was unusual for a mere lieutenant colonel. General Poor was on furlough, as was his second in command, Colonel Cilley. Of the three remaining colonels, Hale of the 2nd New Hampshire had been taken prisoner, and Scammel of the 3rd New Hampshire had been promoted to adjutant general and had moved to Washington's headquarters in Middlebrook. Reid, of the 2nd New Hampshire and successor to Colonel Hale, is unaccountably missing from the muster rolls for Camp Redding. Of the lieutenant colonels, Dearborn ranked below Antil, who was a prisoner of war, and Reid, who had been detached on special duty. Thus, Dearborn was literally left in charge.

He would only command for two weeks, and during that time, the New Hampshire regiments were divided into divisions of one hundred men, as Hazen's men had been earlier, and division by division marched on in subsequent days to Peekskill. Life for the commander was not without its diversions. On April 9, he commented, "We had a Desent Dance at my quarters which we consider as the last we shall have this year." By April 11, he noted that the last of the brigades had marched out of camp. He himself marched for Peekskill on the thirteenth, arriving there the next day. He found his troops quartered in huts in the Highlands just north of Peekskill, presumably those left by the troops who had camped there for the winter.

The removal of the New Hampshire Brigade happened over a month and a half before the Connecticut men were marched out of the center and west camps. It appears that even this early, Washington had plans for the New Hampshire men to take part in a campaign to the west. For over a year, there had been a series of raids by the Iroquois against settlers in western New York state and in the valley of the Susquehanna River under the encouragement of their British allies. These raids had been conducted with such a fury of massacre and destruction that Congress ordered the army to run a series of retaliatory raids. Their instructions were to destroy all Indian villages and crops belonging to the Six Nations and to engage the Indian and Tory marauders to the greatest extent possible, driving them so far west that future raids would be impossible. This expedition, which was under the command of Major General John Sullivan, lasted more than three months during the summer of 1779 and very successfully ended the Indian terror in that region until after the Revolution.

How to Leave a Winter Camp

The summer's fighting season was not begun by just marching out of camp. Although there is very little documentation concerning the preparation for vacating the east camp, the removal of the Connecticut troops from the center and west camps was considerably more leisurely and was accompanied by a flurry of orders that cast light on what an army required in order to move and also what the camps were like.[99]

Of immediate concern was cleaning the camps. By orders of April 12, all of the surgeons were to meet and devise the most effective methods for cleaning the huts, as well as the overall camp, to preserve the health of the soldiers with the onset of warmer weather. Four days later, the officers were admonished to look after the health of their troops and, toward that end, to see that clothes were neat and clean. The huts were to be cleaned from dirt and filth and opened to admit a fair circulation of fresh air through them. Further, a party from each regiment was to be paraded to the quartermaster's "to bury the dead Carcasses Offals of the Cattle and other Substance of filth in the Vicinity of Camp whereby putrefying will endanger the health of the Troops, & to provide Vaults near the Camp which are every morning to be covered with fresh earth."

The "vaults" in this case refer to the sanitary facilities for the camps, and to date these have not been located. Sanitation, specifically the handling of septic waste, remains one of the areas of camp life about which we know precious little. Occasionally, orders were issued dictating that soldiers were only to relieve themselves in the facilities (vaults) supplied for that purpose, suggesting that it was common to avoid the walk to the proper facilities in the cold weather and instead relieve oneself in the vicinity of the huts. Unfortunately, nowhere in these orders is there any hint of how far away these facilities were nor how they were located with respect to the camps' freshwater supplies.

These orders, coming only toward the end of the encampments, show that there was a general lack of concern over sanitation, possibly because it was assumed that cold weather mitigated against the generation of disease. The warmth within the huts, however, meager that it may have been, would have served to create an unhealthy atmosphere, but there was obviously no thought of airing them out until the weather became warm and the surgeons were ordered to come up with suggestions for more healthful procedures. The odoriferous qualities of the huts, as well as the areas of camp where animals were slaughtered, must have added an atmosphere that even modern reenactors' demand for realism has not been able to capture.

Another class of orders was issued to prepare soldiers for the coming fighting season. As early as April 12, the camp's noncommissioned officers were to inspect the troops under their command to assess the number of usable flints that each possessed. They were then ordered to draw up a return that would ensure that each man had three when he marched out. Ten days later, a further series of returns was to be submitted regarding the arms and accoutrements that were wanting to bring the troops up to full fighting status. These returns were also to be submitted to the quartermaster, who was to supply the deficiencies. It appears that there was no shortage of weapons and the supplies to keep them in firing condition.

It may have been during this period that the enlisted men made the small fire pits used to cast musket balls, but the only evidence for this is the archaeological discoveries that we made in the enlisted men's huts. There are no orders concerning this, but it would make sense that they would have been casting ammunition as they attempted to bring themselves up to a fighting strength of thirty cartridges per man. The process of obtaining powder and paper to make cartridges is, at present, unknown, as are the men who were responsible for making cartridges.

Another series of orders dealt with an entirely different problem of preparedness. Over the course of the winter, the usual camp duties were performed, but exercising the troops was apparently neglected. On April 22, the following order was given:

> *It is now a season of the year in which the exercise of the Troops may with conveniency be attended upon—the Troops therefore in camp and not on Duty will for the future exercise from five to seven oClock in the morning and from four to six in the afternoon daily. The Adjut. of the Several Regts. will have their men on the Brigd. Parade precisely at that time. The Brigd. Inspector will then take charge of them and pursue the established rules of exercise for the Army and direct the necessary Maneuvers as there is but a small Number of men in camp at present.*

"Exercise" in eighteenth-century military parlance meant rehearsal of the various coordinated maneuvers that soldiers were expected to perform in battle. These maneuvers were to be found in the "Manual of Arms" that Baron von Steuben had written the previous winter in Valley Forge, which was responsible for turning the American rebels into an efficient army capable of resisting British regulars in the field. It was very successful, as British general Clinton found at the Battle of Monmouth the following spring. The discipline to perform these battle maneuvers had apparently lapsed over the previous four months, and in preparing to embark on the fighting season of 1779, some measure of organization had to be regained.

It is instructive to note the comment in these orders regarding the "small number of men in camp at present." The detached duties of the previous months had contributed to this shortage. Part of the preparation for departure was to get the men back, and many orders were issued to that effect. Advertisements were even put in the state's newspapers that the soldiers delegated to the Redding camps were due back in all haste.[100]

A series of orders dated to late April points to yet another continuing problem in the winter camps, especially when it came time to decamp: shortage of wagons. Putnam had begun to issue a series of requests in mid-April for wagons and horse teams to Nehemiah Hubbard, who was in charge of procuring supplies and equipment for the Connecticut troops. These requests were then sent in turn to Nathanael Greene, the quartermaster general of the Continental army then at his headquarters at Middlebrook. In reply, Greene sent a noncommittal answer and reminded Hubbard that "Washington will not permit use of soldiers as wagoners." Greene then urged Hubbard to enlist those needed and suggested recruiting "a number of good honest farmers as wagon masters." Greene then promised to allow them "Twelve Pounds a Month, Pennsylvania money, and a suit of clothes."[101]

One of those local farmers was James Sanford, who had been serving as a teamster for the east camp all winter and who was one of the eyewitnesses to the executions of Smith and Jones. According to him:

> *When said Brigade dicamped and took up their line of March in April 1779 they went into the state of New York at the Fishkills on the North* [Hudson] *River and pitched their tents at what was called Soldiers Fortune, a place about four miles south of Fishkill landing…I volunteered my services and went with my team with said Brigade in the state of New York…and continued in said team service under the command of Capt. Simson who was then a conductor or superintendent of the teams or baggage wagons until the 5th of June 1779 when my time of service expired.*[102]

Another attempt to meet the wagon shortage was a sequence of orders regarding officers' baggage issued on April 23 and repeated the next day. The orders explicitly stated, "The Officers are directed to disencumber themselves of all heavy Baggage as they will be allowed to only carry such as is indispensably necessary—the Officers of every Department will pay the strictest attention to this order and exert their utmost endeavors to have everything in greatest readiness that there may be no delay in marching." It was promised that the possessions the officers were to jettison would be transported to them at a later date, but there is no confirmation that the original orders were followed or that the promises were ever kept.

With all of the preparatory orders and exercises of late April, as well as the constant insistence that the soldiers were to be ready to march at a moment's notice, the Connecticut regiments were remarkably late in abandoning Redding. Brigade orders to march were finally issued on May 29, and the next day, Parsons's orders to his troops were addressed at Ridgefield. By May 31, they were camped near Fishkill, as Sanford remarked. From here, they took part in the very successful attack and capture of the fortifications at Stony Point under General Anthony Wayne.

The Fate of the Huts: The Documentary Evidence

Among the preparatory orders issued on April 1, before Dearborn departed the east camp, one was a surprise that has forced us to revise our view of how the camps were abandoned. According to the park guides written by Charles Burr Todd in the early years of the twentieth century, the log huts were burned as the troops marched out of the camps, leaving cleared land.[103] This seemed to be confirmed with our excavation of the first enlisted men's hut when we discovered an abundance of charcoal and fire-baked rock littering the level of the hut's dirt floor.

The discovery of Joel Smith's orderly book, however, indicated that this terminal scenario was not correct. Orders specifically stated that the officers were to see that "no injury is to be done to the Hutts which are or may be evacuated that neither the doors laths or floors or any part of them are destroyed so as to prevent their being converted into Hospitals or any other purpose for which they are proper and may be wanted." It will be remembered that this order led us to reevaluate this first excavated hut and also led us to believe that it had been one of the huts turned into a hospital. According to the muster rolls, twenty-seven New Hampshire men were listed as "sick in camp" in April 1779, the month when those troops left camp. (The month before, when the Canadian troops left, fifteen men were so listed.[104]) At the normal occupancy of twelve men per hut, this would mean that at least four huts in what is today the park were probably set aside for the purpose of convalescence. It is not certain how long these huts were so used, but for several months we can assume that some men continued to lived on the park grounds.

The fate of all the huts can be guessed by examining the fate of the huts at Morristown the next winter, for which we have better documentation. Just as the orders were issued by Putnam for the Redding camps, orders were issued for the preservation of the huts inhabited by the Maryland and New Jersey regiments.[105] Trouble maintaining the huts, however, soon developed. In a series of letters written by Quartermaster Joseph Lewis to General Greene starting in July, he complained, "The huts that are evacuated will soon be stripped of Boards by thieves…wish for your directions on how to deal with them." A week later, he is more specific: "The boards and nails are daily taken from the huts by the inhabitants who say they have bought them from the officers who lived in the huts…I am of the opinion they had no right to dispose of them but wait your orders to detain them."[106]

Lewis stopped the thefts and appointed a panel to put a value on the timber and other construction materials used in the huts, as well as to deal with the various claims made against the army for land use and material used by the soldiers. In a follow-up letter by Lewis dated July 9, 1780, he explained: "[B]ecause many of the inhabitants chose to keep the Hutts standing on their land in part pay for the damage they have sustained I have deferred the disposal of them until the Commissioners meet to determine their value."[107] It appears, therefore, that the buildings constructed for the Morristown winter camp became compensation for the landowners for the use of their land and the wood that had been cut.

No similar documentation has yet been found pertaining to the theft of hut hardware and boards at the Putnam encampment, and in fact, there may not have been any. The ownership of the land in the case of the Redding camp was simpler than at Morristown, where the encampment areas were composed of parcels of land from several different owners. The east camp in Redding under Putnam's command was owned by one person, John Read. Colonel Read, therefore, is the primary person the army had to deal with after the 1778–79 winter encampment. The day after the New Hampshire men marched away, the following orders were issued:

> *Head Qts Redding April 12th 1779*
>
> *Capt. Lt. Barns of the 8th Conn. Battallion is apointed to attend at Col. Reades tomorrow Morning 10 o'clock to assist in Prising Some Damages Done to Col. Reades Land by a Brigd. Encamping on it Last winter other Gentlemen will meat him att the same time for that Purpose.*[108]

The results of the commission were passed on to Nehemiah Hubbard, who was perplexed as to how to proceed with compensating Read for the damage done to his property. There followed a series of letters leading to Greene's final judgment that for damages done to farmers by the army, Congress allowed for "no damages at all." Greene went on to tell Hubbard, however, that he can reimburse those farmers for goods taken for use of the army as long as "the public is not imposed upon."

In a series of orders dated May 12 and May 20, a commission was set up to consider the claims of various Redding farmers and, if found worthy, to issue pay warrants.[109] This commission, however, only considered claims for "Articals taken for use of the Troops." It did not consider compensation for the use of the land. Presently, documents have not been found that give the results of the April 12 commission, which was charged to meet with Colonel Read for this purpose. Considering the army's lack of money, and the intrinsic value that winter encampment huts possessed, it is reasonable to assume that the huts were turned over to Read in compensation for the use of the land and the damages done to it. This would have established the precedent for similar action the next year at Morristown.

For John Read and his family, then, the Putnam encampment huts constituted a rich source for board lumber, nails, window glass and a copious supply of logs, which would have become many cords of firewood. These resources were probably harvested from the huts over a period of several years. John Read, for a fee, may have allowed other local residents to partake of these resources as well.

THE FATE OF THE HUTS: THE ARCHAEOLOGICAL EVIDENCE

The documentary evidence for hut deconstruction appears to account for an orderly mining of the resources left by the soldiers. This, however, appears to be contradicted by the archaeological evidence for heavy burning. The signs of burning were very clear in the first enlisted men's hut that we excavated, but if our speculation is correct that this hut was recycled as a hospital after the troops left, it quite possibly may have been burned for sanitation reasons when the last patient either was moved out or died. Although it is not as robust, evidence of burning also exists for the other two enlisted men's huts, as well as the officer's quarters. The remains were definitely engulfed in flames sometime after the end of their useful lives.

The answer to this contradiction may lie in the way in which the huts were salvaged. If the hut logs were harvested over the course of several years, many of the logs would have begun to decay. Once that happened, they would have been deemed unusable even for firewood. Therefore, once the usable wood was cleared from the site, the remaining debris was cleared away by burning, leaving the charcoal and traces of fire-baked rock that we were finding.

This pattern of salvage would also account for the lack of evidence of sills for the hut walls. If the huts had simply been allowed to decay, the sill (or lowest tier of logs used to support the log superstructure) would have rotted out, leaving rich organic material in the form of soil discolorations usually in the shape of the rotted log (a log mold). As mentioned previously, log molds were absent in all of the enlisted men's huts, forcing us to rely on bone scatter to locate the shadow of the hut walls.

An exception to this was found in the south wall of the officer's quarters, where there was a distinct circular soil discoloration six to seven inches in diameter and filled with fragments of charcoal. The presence of this log mold tends to confirm the salvage scenario. The roof boards were most likely salvaged first since they were finished lumber and therefore usable for other building purposes. They were considerably more valuable than the log walls, which were not usable for much more than firewood. Once removed, the hut was vulnerable to precipitation in the form of rain and snow. After a couple of years, the roofless structure would have been subject to considerable water damage. Since the land on which the officer's quarters was built sloped downward to the south, water would have run off to the south and accumulated against the sills of the south wall. This would have led to their rapid deterioration. The now rotten logs would have been left as the rest of the logs were salvaged. Thus it became part of the remainder of the hut that was burned off. The least rotten parts of the sill were easily combustible and became the charcoal fragments. The more rotted section resisted burning and continued to decay into discolored soil in the shape of the original logs.

Another indication of salvage activity was the nails. Only four hand-wrought nails typical of eighteenth-century construction were recovered in the first enlisted men's hut, but more than 115 were found in the officer's quarters, 26 of which were recovered in the smaller fireplace. Many of these nails were found around the periphery of the officer's private room, suggesting that they were used to hold down floorboards, one of the luxuries allowed an officer and denied to the lower ranks, who spent the winter on dirt floors.

A careful examination of the nails showed that seven of them exhibited the graceful curve that comes from having been pulled out of a piece of wood with a claw hammer. These nails clearly show the evidence that the floorboards, which were valuable finished lumber, as were the roof slabs, were carefully salvaged. One puzzle remains. Nails were also a valuable commodity. Why were they not salvaged with the boards?

The large number of nails found in the fireplace may also be an indication of salvage. Their presence suggests that as the building was deconstructed, pieces of useless lumber would have been consigned to the fireplace, where they would have been incinerated along with the other useless remains of the hut. Some of these nails had been hammered over at ninety degrees to the main axis, as if they had been clinched to join two fairly thin boards. These were obviously not worth the effort to straighten and thus were not salvaged, but this still leaves us with the mystery of why the straighter nails were not removed from the fireplace after the wood had been burned away.

From both documentary and archaeological perspectives, the fate of the huts has gradually become clearer, giving us insight into the nature of these buildings when they were still standing. No longer do we see a landowner, in this case John Read, wastefully burning off a large standing supply of firewood but rather salvaging everything of value in a typically frugal Yankee fashion.

THE EFFECT OF THE WINTER ENCAMPMENTS ON REDDING

By the time that Hawkins and Dearborn had moved into the wooded valley that would later become Putnam Park, and their Connecticut counterparts had settled in the center and west camps, the population of Redding had increased at least threefold, from a farming population of about 1,500 inhabitants to over 4,500.[110] This population increase literally occurred overnight, and its impact was felt almost immediately and most notably on the town's resources of food, forage and timber. It surely must have been a great temptation to raid the fences of neighboring farms for construction material rather than to cut your own. It was only the constant threat of courts-martial that maintained the minimal discipline necessary to kept this from happening, but the orderly books and archaeology show that pilferage did occur.

Initially, however, the prospect of having the army in town over the winter was more positive than negative. The army provided protection. Memories were not so short that the inhabitants did not remember the British raid of the year before that had resulted in the destruction of personally property, as well as military stores, especially in Danbury. When contemplating the compensation that should be given to citizens who suffered damage as a result of the winter camps, Nathanael Greene's opinion was that "the protection they give is always considered an equivalent for the inconveniences…[and] the Dung that is left on the ground are objects of some consequences."[111] In addition, the proximity of an army has always been good for business, as soldiers buy things from the locals that make their lives a little easier. In the Redding case, however, the shortage of even badly inflated cash due to infrequently being paid would not have made this a strong advantage to the local economy.

Not everyone was pleased by the prospect of a nearby winter camp. Redding had a strong Anglican church, founded almost fifty years before. The very nature of this Church of England, with the king as its head and the weekly prayers said for his health, was conducive to Loyalist sentiments. The region of Redding Ridge was so notoriously Loyalist that the state could not trust the local militia company and had to disband it shortly after the beginning of hostilities, distributing the few Patriot members to the western company. These Loyalist residents could not have been very happy about a rebel presence in their midst.

Regardless of the initial positive sentiments toward the camps, as the winter progressed the relations between the military and civilian populations became strained. Pilfering did occur. Although there is little documentation for this, there is archaeological evidence in the faunal remains that were recovered. Bird bones were found in several areas of the excavated hut floors, but poultry was never a part of the diet supplied by the army. The bones, of course, could have been water fowl, but the restrictions against wanton discharge of firearms would make this less likely than them being the result of foraging expeditions by soldiers trying to supplement diets that were occasionally strained by scarcity. Unauthorized foraging expeditions were common and mentioned frequently in memoirs and diaries.[112] Even though those for the Redding camps do not mention them, it is highly unlikely that they did not occur, and local farmers bore the brunt of these activities.

The discontent that built up over the winter was dealt with in the usual military manner—a committee was formed. On May 20, just a couple of days before the final regiments left town, there was a general order

> *to facilitate the settlement of the accounts which any of the Inhabitants may have against the Public for wood, timber or other articles taken for the use of the Troops the winter past—The General directs that a committee*

> *be appointed consisting of three persons two of which to be Field Officers and the other a good Substantial Inhabitant to examine into the Demands for things taken for the use of the Army & to give certificates at the Foot of the Accounts…Directed to the QM General or his Deputies which will serve as warrants to pay upon.*

Regrettably, the resulting accounts of this committee have not survived; it would have served as a list of the civilian grievances against the army.

Ironically, the next order after the one forming the committee was to inform the troops that Zalmon Read (Colonel John Read's brother) "yesterday [lost] a Silver pint Cup marked on the outside W.B. Whoever will return it to the owner or leave it with the Brigade Major Shall receive ten Dollars and no questions asked." There is no indication that Mr. Read ever recovered his property.

Probably the most profound effect was not the use of resources, since most of those would be replaced over time, but rather the attachments that occurred as the result of interactions between soldiers and civilians, especially female civilians. These social interactions are not well understood. There must have been dances and other opportunities to meet with civilians in Redding, but there is virtually no documentation of them. The only evidence for such socializing was found by Charles Burr Todd in the records of the Congregational Church kept by Reverend Nathaniel Bartlett. Between February 7 and May 23, 1779, there were eight marriages between women of the parish and soldiers.[113] In addition, as a result of later pension depositions, we know of two women from Newtown who married soldiers from the east camp—for one, we have been able to reconstruct the details of the courtship.

A WAR BRIDE CASE STUDY: BETSEY FOOT

The discovery of Betsey Foot's story came from a footnote in Holly Mayer's book *Belonging to the Army*, a well-documented study of the relationship between civilians and soldiers during the Revolution. In her chapter on liaisons that resulted in marriage was this note: "Betsey Foot…met her future husband at a ball where locals and soldiers mingled in Newtown, Connecticut, in January 1779."[114] This statement had been derived from pension documents, the copies of which we were able to obtain from the National Archives. In the file were depositions that were taken from two of the wedding guests and a long deposition from Betsey Foot Hewes made in

1836, giving the story of her relationship and marriage to Samuel Hewes in her own words.[115]

In 1760, Betsey, one of nine children, was born in the Taunton section of Newtown to George and Catherine Foot. The Taunton district was located along the eastern border with Danbury (later Bethel) about three miles from Putnam Memorial Park, where Samuel Hewes was camped that winter with the 1st New Hampshire Regiment. In January, Betsey, who was then eighteen, attended a dance in Newtown with some of her girlfriends to which several New Hampshire soldiers had also been invited, including Sam and some of his camp mates. The presence of an exotic and exciting uniformed stranger quickly attracted Betsey to the young soldier, or maybe it was the other way around. Regardless, shortly after their meeting, Betsey received a letter from Hewes asking to "receive his address." With the advice and urging of her brother, Abel, she agreed, and the two began seeing each other on a fairly regular basis, or at least regular enough that by the end of March, they had "engaged to be married and our publishment had been written."

At this point, the story takes on an unfortunate twist. George Foot was a faithful Anglican, which meant that he was a Loyalist, and the thought of his daughter marrying an American soldier threw him into a rage of tremendous proportions. It appears, however, that brother Abel did not share his father's sentiments. In 1777, he had taken the oath of loyalty to the new government and was thus in sympathy with the efforts of the Continental Congress. This explains why he was so willing to advise his sister to meet with Hewes and to promote their liaison.

Since Hewes was due to march out of camp with his regiment in early April, there was little time to arrange and perform the marriage. Betsey's father, therefore, prevailed on his prospective son-in-law to postpone the marriage until after the next season of campaigning, which Hewes reluctantly agreed to do. The word had gone out that the New Hampshire troops were to be attached to General Sullivan's expedition to avenge the Indian depredations in western New York and Pennsylvania. Since this campaign was to be a rough and dangerous one, Mr. Foot hoped that Hewes would prove to be one of the casualties, as he later admitted to his daughter.

Unfortunately for the elder Foot, the campaign was successful, with few casualties. In the third week in November 1779, Hewes was back in the area with the rest of the New Hampshire troops to again guard the military stores at Danbury. It appears that the old camp quarters occupied the previous winter were no longer available, probably because the salvage process had already begun, so they camped near what is today the western border of Bethel with Newtown. This put Hewes less than a mile and a half from his fiancée. George Foot's opposition to the marriage had been thwarted, and the date for the wedding was set for December 16.

From the deposition of two Newtown men who had been wedding guests, we have some rare details of the nuptials. They took place at the Foot home and were to have been presided over by Reverend John Beach, one of the most prominent Anglican clergymen in Fairfield County and a man who had founded the churches in Redding and Newtown. He was also one of the oldest, being in his late seventies.

Although all of the guests made it safely to the Foot home, there was a severe snowstorm and Reverend Beach, because of his advanced years, felt that he could not make the four-mile journey from the rectory to the wedding site. Hewes and his bride then decided that if the minister could not come to the wedding, then the wedding would go to the minister, or at least part of it would. Accordingly, at four o'clock in the afternoon, the bride and groom, along with three other couples who would act as witnesses, squeezed into a sleigh and made the trip to Beach's. Included among the witnessing couples were John Kinney, a friend and fellow soldier, and a local girl who he would later marry. Regrettably, her name has not survived. After the ceremony, they all returned to Betsey's house for the wedding's social festivities. Unfortunately, in the confusion, no one thought of recording the wedding. This was the reason for the flurry of paperwork in 1836 in an attempt to establish that it did in fact happen.

In the immediate aftermath of the wedding, Hewes was required to return to camp since he was still a corporal in the New Hampshire line. Betsey, it appears, did not care to become a camp follower and join her new husband in camp, so she remained at home and he came to be with her as often as he could get away. This situation did not last very long. Since he had enlisted in 1777 for a term of three years, his enlistment was over on April 22, 1780, so he was honorably discharged four months after the wedding, after which he moved in with Betsey in the Foot homestead. This situation must have lasted five or six months, because Peter Fairchild, one of the deposed witnesses, remembered that she had a child who was born in Newtown.

This was not a happy time for either Hewes or his wife: "My father's opposition was violent against Hewes because he was a soldier, so that he was frequently turned out of doors and I was compelled to leave my father's house by the influence of the Tories. But I was determined not to yield to the point and so persevered unto the end."

It would be pleasant to write that there was a happy ending and that they lived happily ever after, but such apparently was not the case. We know very little about the subsequent events of their lives, but we do know that they finally left Newtown and returned to Hewes's home in Lyme, New Hampshire. There they lived until Hewes died in 1816. It is uncertain how many children they eventually had besides the one born in Newtown. There is also at least one descendant who gained entrance to the Daughters of the American Revolution (DAR) through him, but that is the limit of our information on the family.

We are not even sure when Betsey died. The agent who had been handling her pension papers claimed that she was in need of the pension because "Mrs. Hewes is very poor and has no permanent home." According to the deposition of Daniel Miller of Windsor, Vermont, he had been "acquainted with Hewes for the past 17 years a great part of which she has resided in my family." Miller does not appear to have been a relative, so it is quite possible that he had taken her in as one of the town's poor, for which he would have been reimbursed. It is known that her pension was granted in 1837 and that it amounted to eighty-eight dollars per year retroactive to 1834, when the pension act had been passed. This must have afforded her some relief, but since she was seventy-seven yeas old when the pension was granted, she probably did not enjoy it for long.

Betsey Foot Hewes's story is not of great importance, but it does illustrate one of the effects that soldiers had on a community during the Revolution. Beyond that, however, it is of value because it humanizes the events of that winter in Redding. Her trials and tribulations take us behind the raw statistics of the Revolution to show that there were real people and very human situations driving them.

The Next Winter: A Footnote to the Park

An intriguing comment in Betsey Foot's deposition was that her husband had returned to Danbury the next winter. Until fairly recently, very little was known about this second winter encampment, and little if any of the site remains intact, but what information we have is a fitting conclusion to the story of the larger Redding camps of the previous winter.

The existence of the 1779–80 winter camp first came to our attention in the memoir of Benjamin Hoyt, which was transcribed and published by Danbury's Scott-Fanton Museum in 1977 as part of that city's national bicentennial celebration.[116] Hoyt was born in 1778, so although too young to remember the winter camp that was occupied when he was a mere two years old, he would have heard firsthand accounts of it from family and older members of the community. His memoir written in 1830, then, is very close to being an eyewitness account. He recorded, "In the winter of 1779 & 1780 a Brigade of New Hampshire troops came into the ground late in the fall a few days before the snow began to fall (for it was a memorable winter called the hard winter) & commenced cutting down the beautiful forest beginning a few rods west of Capt. Benedict's."[117] Benedict was a neighbor of the Hoyts, and with the many references to neighbors and the disposition of the troops that Hoyt mentions, the camp can be located in the Wild Cat section of Bethel, now Elmwood.

There are several documents besides the Hoyt memoir that confirm the existence of the camp and give a little more information about it. One of the most interesting, and completely frustrating, is the journal of Major David Livermore. His record for Thursday, November 2, 1779, reads, "This day I proceeded on the March and go to ground laid out for hutting, which is in the vicinity of Danbury, towards Newtown."[118] The next day, he continued, "[T]hese three days the troops are busy in clearing and fixing for laying foundation of the huts." On Thursday, December 7, he further recorded, "This day I lay the foundation of my hut, twenty two feet in length and twelve in width." (This is one of the only reliable documents relating to the size of officer's quarters.) Regrettably, this is the last entry he makes until April 6, 1780, when he wrote, "After spending a very disagreeable winter in the outskirts of Danbury, bordering on Newtown, at a place called Wild Cat, and going through many disagreeable scenes, which circumstances have prevented my keeping minute of, this day Poor's brigade leave their winter quarters and march for West Point."

One other important clue to locating the camp precisely was in an orderly book kept by one of the brigade captains from November 30 to December 23, 1779.[119] The order for December 1 showed that the officers had learned from the previous year's encampment: "The Troops are not to go south of the field on the right of the encampment to cut wood either for building or for firewood upon Mr. Benjamin Hiccock's land or late Benedict's on any pretense what ever." Obviously, with the complaints of damage due to indiscriminant cutting of wood around the Redding camps, the commanding officers had learned to severely restrict the harvesting of wood resources.

Now armed with the property owners abutting the camp, it was time to spend some time in the Danbury land and with probate records to come up with a more precise location. In this we were partially successful. The search was narrowed down to part of the area in the old Wild Cat School District in Bethel. This district was bounded on the east by the Newtown border and stretched from modern Route 302 north to Plumtrees Road. Its western border was unknown and unimportant. The camp then centered on Old Hawleyville Road probably as far north as Plumtrees Road.

We would not have known the precise layout of the camp if it had not been for the efforts of Bethel's town historian, Pat Wild. He had spent the better part of his summer vacation in obsessive research and had come to a conclusion similar to ours but much more precise. He had actually mapped all of the properties that were mentioned in the various sources and had located the camp southward from Plumtrees Road, just to the west of Old Hawleyville Road. The modern housing development along Vinning Road went right through the center of the camp, destroying what remains may have been there. The southern portion of Blue Jay Orchards had obliterated the rest of it.

The existence of this encampment raises some interesting questions about the location of winter camps, especially in this area. The first and most obvious was why they did not go back to reoccupy the old huts that had been left standing in Putnam Park. Huts were reused elsewhere. The Connecticut huts at Morristown, for example, had been reused for two consecutive winters. As suggested before, the answer to this may lie in the way the Redding huts had been salvaged. Read had quite probably begun to dismantle them.

There is another, even more compelling reason for General Poor to move his troops to the northeast of the old site: it would be in a better position to guard a major east–west artery for the movement of provisions. Washington had carefully guarded this route since it was vital for transporting provisions from eastern Connecticut to the military supply depots in Danbury and then to the west along the Hudson River. Connecticut was well known as the "Provisions State," but all of the provisions in the state would be worthless if they could not be transported westward to the army. Washington was also sensitive to the possible need for a route along which to retreat if the British attacked north along the Hudson River and successfully cut the Continental army in half. He was so concerned about the viability of the road that he even sent engineers to repair and rebuild the bridge across the Housatonic River. That major east–west route, after passing through Newtown, went through Bethel along modern Plumtrees Road, just north of the waiting New Hampshire troops.

CHAPTER 6

The Founding and Development of a State Park in Connecticut

Dearborn and Hawkins had left. The huts stood deserted until the Read family salvaged what they could and burned off the wooden remains. Gradually the valley returned to brushy scrub growth that marks a reemerging forest, except for a small section where crops were planted and vainly encouraged to grow. Apple trees were planted in collapsed remains of the northern chimneys that had served Hazen's Canadian Volunteers, and they continued to flower until the end of the nineteenth century, at which time they were visited by local residents whose grandparents told of the encampment that had passed into local folklore.

By 1880, a new antiquarian interest was being shown in the old east campgrounds. In the first edition of his history of Redding, written in that year, Charles Burr Todd described the remains as they then appeared:

> *The ruins if the first* [east] *camp are most distinct, and form perhaps one of the best preserved, as well as most interesting, relics of the Revolution within the reach of the antiquary…The camp was until recently covered with heavy forests, which explains perhaps the secret of its preservation. The present owner is clearing up the underbrush which has overgrown the ruins, rendering it easy of access to visitors, and it will in time no doubt become a favorite place of resort.*[120]

The south end of the Company Street, showing how it looked in 1887 at the time the park land was purchased and before the landscaping began.

CHARLES BURR TODD AND CONNECTICUT'S FIRST STATE PARK

Charles Burr Todd was the prime moving force behind the creation and preservation of Putnam Memorial State Park. Unfortunately, little is known of his personal life, and no photo of him survives. He was born in 1849 in Redding and appears to have wanted a career as a schoolteacher, but his eyes were too weak to sustain this occupation, and he turned instead to be a freelance writer, although it is doubtful that this profession was much easier on his eyes. He is known to have published articles concerning local history in several prominent late nineteenth-century magazines including *Lippincott's Monthly Magazine*, the *Youth's Companion*, the *Magazine of American History* and the *New York Evening Post*. Several of his articles of antiquarian interest to citizens of Connecticut were gathered and republished under the cumbersome title *In Olde Connecticut: Being a Record of Quaint, Curious and Romantic Happenings There in Colonial Times and Later.*[121] Similar volumes were produced for Massachusetts and New York.

Todd's attachment to his hometown and his own heritage led him to write *The True Aaron Burr*, from whom he traced descent. His fascination with Joel Barlow, who had grown up in Redding to become one of the country's first literary figures, as well as an early statesman, led him to publish the *Life and Letters of Joel Barlow*, the first biography of this obscure man. It was this attempt to raise his visibility in the nation's consciousness that led him to insist that a memorial circle be created in the park, even though Barlow had no association with the camp during the Revolution. Todd's posthumous triumph in this regard came in 1956, when the regional high school for the towns of Easton and Redding was named Joel Barlow High School.

His near obsession with the history of his hometown led him to write its history in 1880 along with brief genealogies of its native families with whom he was almost equally obsessed. This was updated twenty-five years later with a second, much expanded edition. In this he included much more material on the Redding camps that had been discovered in the years since the first edition, including an account of the formation of the park. He was thus a leading force in the creation of the park by virtue of his reputation as the area's leading historian.

It was Isaac Bartram, however, who actually began the park forming process. He had grown up in Redding and had been a friend and schoolmate of Todd's but had moved to Sharon, where he became involved in business and the local politics of that corner of the state. In 1886, he was elected to the General Assembly, and in the fall of that year, he wrote a letter to Todd telling him that he had been stimulated by Todd's description of the winter encampment in his history of Redding and that he intended to propose to the January 1997

Isaac N. Bartram, member of the state legislature from Sharon and the park founder, supervising the construction of the main entrance in 1890. *Courtesy of the Sharon Historical Society.*

session a bill that would have the state obtain the campground as a perpetual memorial to the local soldiers of the Revolution. To facilitate this, he suggested that Todd approach Aaron Treadwell about the donation or sale of the camp lands that he owned, which at this time he was using only as a cow pasture.

It was Todd, then, who secured Aaron Treadwell's agreement to donate his twelve-acre tract that contained forty-five of the hut remains to the state, provided that it be used as a memorial to Israel Putnam and the soldiers who wintered there. This offer was transmitted to the state's General Assembly along with Bartram's proposal, and the assembly immediately formed a committee to visit and report on the site, which was done with great local fanfare on February 3. With Todd as a guide and with suitable wining and dining in Danbury, the committee reported back to the assembly on February 9 that the site was indeed as Bartram and Todd had described it in their petition—a worthy antiquarian landmark for preservation as a state memorial. Accordingly, on April 1, a resolution was passed, and Treadwell's gift became Connecticut's first state park. Governor Lounsbury then signed it into law.

Interestingly, Todd was vehemently opposed to the creation of a "state park" since the term implied frivolity and recreation, which he felt was demeaning to a piece of property that was meant to commemorate the courageous men who had fought for and won our independence.[122] He felt that it should be the Putnam Memorial Campground. Over the years, the words "state" and "park" have variously crept back into the official name of the memorial, until today's official name: Putnam Memorial State Park.

The memorial campground had been formed, but one serious shortcoming had arisen: Treadwell's donation was only about half of the old Company Street—the other half and the auxiliary areas, including what would later be called the cemetery and the powder magazine, lay to the west and north on property still owned by descendants of the Read family. This shortcoming was overcome with the charity of others who had become as fascinated and involved with the commemorative project as Todd had. Oliver Jennings of Fairfield, for example, purchased forty acres to the north that contained the remaining enlisted men's huts from the Read family and immediately donated it to the state. Isaac Bartram purchased another twenty-three acres to the east containing the property that would include the Overlook and later the museum, and this was added to the previous benefactions. At about this time, a twenty-five-acre tract of woodland to the northeast was threatened by logging. Todd approached Jennings again, and he instructed Todd to purchase it in his name, which was done. After Jennings's death, the heirs donated the tract to the park, bringing the total acreage of the park to more than one hundred and thus protecting the campground in its entirety.

As a part of the bill creating the park, a modest $1,800 was included for the construction of a proper memorial marker to be placed in a prominent place at the main entrance. It was going to eventually cost another $20,000 to develop the park, but the small sum would be enough for the first step. As the sum was appropriated, a commission was created by the governor that consisted of those who had been most instrumental in creating the memorial park, namely Banks Gorham of Redding, Isaac Bartram, Aaron Treadwell and C.B Todd. At their first meeting, three of the members professed busy schedules, and so the burden of secretary, and forming the special committee to erect the monument, fell squarely on the shoulders of Todd.[123]

Todd quickly contacted an old friend of his, John Ward Stimson, who was the director of art schools for the Metropolitan Museum of New York City, and engaged him to come up with an appropriate design. These two men had toured the Great Lakes together the previous year, visiting various French and Indian War sites, which gave them inspiration for the layout of the park, but Stimson developed a plan for the monument that was clearly in line with the current fashion for Victorian memorials based around an obelisk. This monumental shape had been developed by the ancient Egyptians.

The monument was the first feature built, and it became the focal point of the memorial park. The cannon in the foreground was one of four pieces of Civil War surplus ordnance given to the park in 1896.

With the deciphering of hieroglyphics in the nineteenth century leading to spectacular discoveries of Egyptian royal life, a fascination with all things Egyptian developed in the West. With this, the obelisk became especially popular for memorials, from the stately Washington Monument to expensive family burial markers in local nineteenth-century cemeteries. Obelisks had also become popular in Revolutionary War memorials, having been used at Bunker Hill and at Fort Griswold in Groton, Connecticut, among other sites.

With the help of architect Walter Briggs of Bridgeport and contractor Philo Bates of Norwalk, local granite was cut and fashioned into an obelisk ten feet square at the base, rising to a height of forty-three feet with a two-and-a-half-foot (diameter) granite ball at its peak. To fit the rustic atmosphere of the landscaping, the masonry was rusticated ashlar as opposed to the smoothly finished masonry of monuments such as Washington's. On the base were smooth granite panels, five feet square and weighting two tons apiece. These came from Ridgefield and contained an inscription that Todd composed. On the west face:

Erected
To Commemorate
The Winter Quarters
Of Putnam's Division
Of the Continental Army
November 7 1778–May 25 1779

On the east face:

The Men of '76
Who suffered here
To preserve forever their
Memory,
The State of Connecticut
Has erected this monument
A.D. 1888

On the north face:

The World
Is full of their praises
Posterity
Stands astonished at their
Deeds.

On the south side, the names of the principal commanders:

Putnam
McDougal
Poor
Parsons
Huntington

The building of the monument was begun in the fall of 1887 and was completed by the summer of 1888.

After the triumph of getting the monument erected, Todd continued to serve on the commission as secretary and remained actively involved in searching out more documentary material on the winter encampment. This, along with his literary proclivities, made him the logical candidate to write a guide to the park, which he did in 1890. This small guide included the Revolutionary War history as it was then known, as well as a description of the features of the memorial. Also included was a long list of relics that had been recovered from the grounds

The park commissioners in 1902 posed in front of the entrance. It was the vision of these men that guided the park in its first three decades.

during landscaping, as well as a number of eighteenth-century artifacts from private donors that were given to swell the campground's growing collection. The guide went through numerous rewrites and enlargements as more was learned about the Redding camps and more relics were recovered. The total number of editions is unknown, but it continued to be reprinted until at least 1927.

Todd resigned from the second commission in 1893 to devote himself to other literary pursuits, including a massive rewrite and updating of his pivotal history of Redding in 1906. Not much is known about his later life. As he became older, however, he moved away from town, living successively in Florida, California and finally in New Jersey at Washington's Crossing. In this last location, he continued his research into the Revolutionary period and produced a guide for that notable historical location. He was apparently living with a nephew here and was indigent. In a pathetic letter of December 10, 1927, written to Governor John H. Trumbull, he pleaded his case for a stipend from the state based on his never having been paid for the many guides that he wrote for the park. In those letters, he outlined his impecunious circumstances.[124] There is no record that his letters were ever answered before his death at age seventy-nine in 1928. He requested that his ashes be buried at the park, but the commission denied this, and he was interred in the family plot on Redding Ridge. A commemorative plaque, however, was cast in bronze and placed in the wall of the Overlook in front of the present park museum in 1931.[125]

THE DEVELOPMENT OF THE MEMORIAL

Todd's plans for the park's development were laid out even before the first visit of the legislative committee in 1887. They started with the monument, which would be the centerpiece of the main entrance, and a year after the monument was finished, an appropriation of $20,000 was forthcoming from the legislature so that the construction of a proper memorial park could begin on July 19, 1889.

The original main entrance of the encampment had probably been the trail that leads into the northwest corner of the park from Chestnut Ridge Road, but in Todd's conception, the main entrance would lead into the southeast corner of the park, off Lonetown Road. Such an entrance location would allow visitors to enter from Redding along an established road. It was hoped that the old Sherman Turnpike that extended from Lonetown Road into Bethel would be rebuilt by the state since it led to the end of a Bethel trolley line at the corner of Routes 58 and 302. This would make a trip from the Bethel train station much shorter and easier.

There was also the relic of a roadbed that ran through a cleft in the rock crags and that led from the southernmost chimney remains eastward to where the artillery park may have been. It was considered by Todd and the rest of the commissioners as a Revolutionary War–era road and was so designated on the survey map that was made at the time of the Treadwell property and filed in the Redding Land Records.[126]

Todd also noted in his early reports that there is a soldier's stone bridge that crossed the stream that drained Lake McDougal and ran through the cleft and into what would later be the reflecting pool. This bridge was considered an important feature of the camp and was marked with granite pillars at each corner to facilitate its preservation. Unfortunately, over the years, the stones of the bridge have become moved, misplaced or lost, as have the corner pillars, so that today we have no idea of the appearance of this bridge. No photographs of it are known. The road, although also considered important, was not as important as having a proper entrance to the park, and so it was sacrificed by being buried under the heavily landscaped main entrance driveway.

To direct the water flowing from the brook that drained Lake McDougal, a culvert was built to carry it under the entrance driveway. In Todd's words,

The park main entrance as it looked in 1909 and still looks today. This image shows how the various elements such as the blockhouses were constructed to frame the view of the monument on the ridge in the back.

The entrance in 1890. The crane is being used to move the stone into what would become the base of one of the blockhouses.

A rare photo of the entrance vista as it looked in the winter of 1936. Although this was a winter encampment, photos of the park in that season are rarely seen.

"[He] would throw over the brook, arched stone parapets such as these troops march over in their campaigns of the Hudson valley." Following that plan, a rough masonry wall was built along the north side of the drive (the south side was flanked by the natural crag), and crenellations were built along the top of that wall.

Flanking each end of the entrance gate is a blockhouse. These stand on ten-foot-square stone bases, with a log superstructure that hangs over the base by two feet on all sides. The log walls were pierced by four loopholes on each side that would have afforded defending soldiers the opportunity to fire at an approaching enemy from a protected vantage point.

There is no evidence that blockhouses were ever built at the campground, but Todd felt that they emphasized the martial nature of the memorial. The model for them had come from his Great Lakes tour, taken the year before the monument was built. During his excursion, he found what he felt to be the only two blockhouses left in existence: one at Sugar Island in the mouth of the Detroit River and the other on Mackinac Island in the Mackinac Straits of northern Michigan. It mattered little that these were both French and Indian War relics; they made a fitting decorative frame for the park's monument. To complete the fortification image, a section of palisade wall extended to the south from the blockhouse to the rock crag and from the other blockhouse north to the adjoining hill.

Once the entrance driveway was finished, a system of gravel roads had to be constructed that would allow visitors access to the various park features. The most important of these ran to the east and alongside the rows of collapsed chimneys from south to north for their entire length. Unfortunately, the construction of this road completely obliterated the parade ground, the area in front of all of the huts on which all of the soldiers would have

The Company Street in 1890 looking south, with Putnam Avenue being constructed over the old parade ground to the left.

Putnam Avenue just finished, with the Company Street to the right and the monument in the distance. The newly made avenue effectively destroyed the old parade ground, which ran in front of the rows of huts when they were standing.

mustered each morning. For a short period during the early park's history, there was also a gravel path that ran between the two rows of stone piles meant to emulate the Company Street, but this appears to have been just a light layer of gravel and was not deeply landscaped, preserving the buried level of the original street almost intact.[127]

Another important road branched off the northern portion of this first street and went east, where it shortly forked into an east and south branch. The east branch then went to the north entrance (which is actually just across the line into Bethel), where there was a miniature version of the blockhouses and gate of the main entrance. The south branch went up a hill to a magnificent point that looks out over the old Sherman Turnpike (now Route 58) and the pond. Here, a stone, paved patio was built that by 1931 held the commemorative bronze plaque honoring Charles Burr Todd. In 1921, the stone museum was built overlooking this patio.

Yet another road extended around the south end of the monument to the west past Lake McDougal. This lake was also constructed by park landscapers and was not a feature of the camp. The brook that ran through this area, however, was original, and it provided water for the New Hampshire solders living in the southern huts. The road then turned to the north, extending all the way to the northwest corner of the park. On the way, it passed the so-

The north or Bethel entrance to the park. This entrance, located at the Bethel end of the park, was built to mimic the main entrance, with its gate and miniature blockhouses.

called cemetery, which was duly noted on all of the early tourist maps and guides. To emphasize the memorial nature of this plot of ground, in 1896 a rough boulder was set on top of a boulder base and inscribed with, "In Memory of the Unknown Heroes Buried Here." At some time in the 1920s, twelve granite posts (with swag chains connecting them) were erected to set the area off as a sacred space. Only since the early 2000s have the signs and guide maps been changed to indicate the true identity of the place as field officer's quarters, but the monument and granite posts remain in memory of the soldiers who died that winter regardless of where they are buried.

With the infrastructure built, efforts and money were turned to interpretation, creating the features of the park that would help the visitor understand the soldier's daily life. This consisted primarily of reconstructing three log buildings in a manner that was thought to be accurate to the time. In fact, they reflect a late Victorian historical mindset that in itself is of interest and is the reason why they have been lovingly preserved and not taken down as our understanding of Revolutionary architecture has advanced.

The first of these is the so-called guardhouse. Documentary evidence has shown that the guardhouse for that winter was not located in any of the camps but rather was on Umpawaug Road. When the park was being set up, however, there were ruins on the hill to the north of the main entrance gate. These were probably the remains of the hut that housed the artillery men, but they were interpreted by the commissioners as the guardhouse. Therefore,

Replica guardhouse built about 1890 on the site of ruins that may have been the remains of the artillery park.

an eighteen- by twelve-foot log building with two windows (originally glazed) was built, with a cute little porch in front of the gable-end door, where presumably a guard could stand out of the rain. Since this building is just two feet longer than the soldiers' huts, it has been outfitted with four stacks of bunks, emulating the cluttered interior of the original huts. Visiting school groups now can be divided into groups of twelve students, who can then be crowded into the hut to experience its claustrophobic nature.

The other two hut reconstructions were likewise built on existing ruins. In the process, they destroyed those remains, so it is impossible to tell what they originally were. The officer's quarters in the northwest corner of the park were built on three existing stone walls that extended back into the hill, leading us to believe that this is actually the powder magazine, as discussed previously. Again, the interpretive markers now reflect this change in interpretation, but the structure has been left, just as the guardhouse has been left, because it is part of the park's Victorian history.

The third hut has had a rougher history. Being located behind the huts lining the Company Street, the ruins on which it was built were interpreted as a company officer's hut, and there is general agreement that this interpretation is correct. It remained where it had been reconstructed until the mid-1970s, when a group of young people was having a party in it. Not realizing that the chimney

Reconstruction of a company officer's quarters that stood behind the Company Street until it was lost to fire in the early 1970s. The chimney of this building still stands at the north end of the Company Street.

was a dummy and did not contain a flue, they managed to burn the hut down when they started a fire in the fireplace. There was an attempt a few years after its destruction to rebuild it using the more accurate knowledge that modern scholarship has given us, but funding ran out and the project was aborted after a few tiers of logs were laid for the walls. Now all that remains is the flueless chimney, which marks the spot where an officer's hut once stood.

By the autumn of 1890, the $20,000 had been spent, and the basic park features were in place, with one exception: the pavilion.[128] In 1893, the year Todd left the commission, work began on this structure, which has the distinction of being the first park building constructed in the state. It was completed in the fall at a cost of $13,000. Its primary purpose was to shelter picnicking visitors to the park from inclement weather. Before the access roads were completed and the automobile was widespread, access to the park required some effort. One did not visit the park for an hour or two but tended to spend a day and eat a meal there. Obviously, bad weather was a problem because there was no place in the park to seek shelter. The pavilion solved that problem in that it provided a roof and sides for shelter, even though the sides were pierced with large lunar openings that were unglazed. Unless the wind was blowing, this building kept the rain off one's picnic food.

There was also a raised clerestory that protruded through the roof and that was serviced by an open staircase that led to its fairly spacious room. This room

The pavilion, with its clerestory, and the reproduction guardhouse to the left. The pavilion was the first park building in the state and was used to take refuge in inclement weather.

was dedicated to the display of relics that had been discovered while the park was being landscaped and quickly developed into a museum. In addition to the displays of eighteenth-century artifacts, the museum attracted donations of antiques from the town and surrounding area. When grandmother died and her house was being cleaned out, the relics of her early life were seen as too valuable to throw out but not of sufficient value to keep. The park museum was remembered, and so the little collection of Revolutionary War relics grew as domestic utensils and antique tools were acquired. The little museum was also seen as a proper place for eighteenth-century antique firearms, and the collection of antiquated weapons grew into a considerable and valuable collection.

By 1921, the commissioners decided that a proper building was needed to house the now large collection with greater security than the pavilion supplied. Hugh McCollum, a Redding contractor, agreed to oversee the work and, by the end of 1921, had constructed a stone replica of a colonial house of one and a half stories. The façade was stone, but the walls, floors, ceilings, foundation and even the roof deck were made of solid, reinforced concrete, making it not only one of the most solid buildings in the northern part of the county but also cool in the summer and warm in the winter—much like a solid stone church houses its precious relics.

In an attempt to improve access to the park, the section of Sherman Turnpike that passed by the entrance and along the east side of the park

The museum building shortly after it was constructed in 1921. This still houses the park's artifacts and relics, although the magnificent collection of firearms was lost to theft in the 1970s.

was finally rebuilt by the Town of Bethel in the mid-1890s as a gravel road. Sometime in the late 1920s, it was repaved with bituminous asphalt by the state and became State Road 58. This allowed easier access from the north for those coming to Bethel by train and then to the new road via trolley. Access from the south, however, remained circuitous. A potential visitor had to pilot his vehicle across Redding Ridge and turn to the west at the junction with Sunset Hill Road, taking what would later be called John Read Road. This was little more than a dirt track through the woods of what was once John Read's farm. From the western intersection of this road with Lonetown Road, one turned right, heading north to the park. By late 1896, a shortcut had been built. The east end of John Read Road was improved and paved with gravel to a point about one-fourth of a mile west of the intersection with Sunset Hill Road. From that point, an entirely new road was laid out and built going northward to the park entrance along the route of modern Route 58.[129]

One final cosmetic touch to the park was added in the summer of 1896. At the beginning of that year, the park personnel were notified that the Boston armory was disposing of surplus Civil War ordnance. The park was offered four thirty-two-pound coastal cannons (used in the coastal artillery) and a quantity of cannonballs, which it accepted.[130] Two of these cannons were mounted on granite blocks flanking the entrance, with two pyramids of cannonballs bolted to a concrete base near each cannon. A third was similarly mounted just below the monument facing and defending the entrance gate. Two pyramids of ammunition were also set up alongside. The fourth was placed defending the northern entrance to the park. They continue to sit in these respective locations, but without their ammunition. As a result of a modern attempt to load one of the cannons, it was deemed prudent by the park staff to remove all of the cannonballs. They were recently rediscovered in the basement of the museum, where they had been taken in the early 1970s.

Another piece of Civil War ordnance was also given to the park and is presently being displayed in the visitors' center: a James Rifle (a 75mm rifled cannon). This was also the subject of some late-night mischief in 1897. J.P. Hill and Dennis Connors were filled with the spirit of the Fourth of July and, according to the local newspaper, filled with other spirits as well. They managed to take the cannon on its wheeled carriage, and a good supply of gunpowder, and run it southward along Lonetown Road, stopping in front of each house to give a salute, sometimes overloading the gun to the point where its report broke windows. When they had exhausted their ammunition, they returned the gun to the park "in a slightly damaged condition." When the park superintendent, Mr. Worthman, heard about the incident, "He was wrathy, and lost no time setting the machinery of the law in Motion." They were apprehended by Constable Bartram, taken to the park, tried and convicted of breach of the peace, resulting in a stiff fine. The reporter's conclusion was that "[t]hey will now learn to be a little more temperate, not only in their patriotism, but their drink."[131] It appears that the desire to find out if the park ordnance is still operable is irresistible.

THE VICISSITUDES OF THE PARK'S FORTUNES IN THE TWENTIETH CENTURY

By 1900, the park had been formed and was established as a place to recreate, have picnics and enjoy group outings, and it also became a place to gather for special occasions. On August 2, 1919, for example, the park became the venue for Redding's celebration welcoming home its World War I veterans. A full day was planned, beginning with athletic games starting at 10:00 a.m. These included a tug of war, a sack race, a rope climb, a one-hundred-yard dash, both running and standing broad jumping and an egg and spoon race, among others. Dinner was held between 12:30 p.m. and 1:30 p.m. in the pavilion and followed by a program of speeches, culminating in the presentation of veterans medals by Lieutenant Governor Clifford Wilson. The program

Children playing on the playground that stood just south of the main entrance in 1931. This is now the location of the main parking lot.

The main entrance of the park in 1919, decked out for the Welcome Home ceremony for Redding's World War I veterans.

concluded with a round of songs, including "Keep the Home Fires Burning," "There's a Long, Long Trail" and "The Battle Hymn of the Republic."

The post-program afternoon was dominated by a baseball game between the Doughboys and the Stay-at-Homes that, as characterized by a reporter,

Sunday school parents and children photographed in 1909 in front of the pavilion. The park was a frequent venue for celebrations and social occasions up through the 1950s. Such visits to the park had diminished until recently.

"promises to be a hummer and, unless we miss our guess, it will be as good as a Charlie Chaplin film…we are wondering who will be the umpire. It will be a dangerous job if the looks of the servicemen is any indication of their real physical condition." The day then ended with a dance at the pavilion, although music had been provided all afternoon and evening along with a steady supply of hot dogs, hamburgers and ice cream cones.[132] This was among the largest public gatherings at the park, but it established the pattern of celebration for the rest of the first half of the century.

Until the Second World War, the park remained an increasingly popular place for picnics and gatherings, especially for church groups and graduating school classes.[133]

This popularity was fed by the increasing prevalence of the automobile during the 1910s and 1920s. The '20s became a golden age of the automobile day trip, and to serve those who enjoyed a refreshing ride into the country, the teahouse phenomenon developed. These were places, often private homes, where one could stop for a light lunch at about noontime before turning back toward home. All of the towns in the interior of Fairfield County had several, although they were ephemeral businesses, usually doing business for only a summer season or two.

A reliable destination for a country drive, and one that could be counted on to always be open during the touring season, however, was the park. Attendance steadily grew into the 1930s. With the onset of the Depression, the park remained popular since it was an inexpensive place at which to spend a pleasant afternoon away from the troubles of the period and the crowded, often grimy condition of the county's cities. It was a refreshing experience combined with the prospects of a historical education that was enhanced when the larger museum building was constructed in 1921, with its informative displays. This, combined with the spectacular display of Revolutionary War ruins, served to bring the visitor into direct contact with history.

The park's prosperity, unfortunately, did not continue to rise as the century moved into its second half. Several factors served to diminish the popularity of the country day trip, not the least of which was the rise of television in the 1950s. Entertainment could now be enjoyed in the home, which tended to isolate people and reduce the social events that the park was so well equipped to serve. The gas shortages of the 1970s also created higher prices for gasoline and a sense of energy conservation that also adversely affected the day-tripping impulse.

Compounding the effects of declining attendance on the park were diminishing state budgets. When funds are scarce, one of the budget areas that was first to be cut was the state parks. Exacerbating this was Connecticut's ignorance of the value of tourism. Rather than pumping money into a historic park that would attract history-minded visitors, money was shunted elsewhere, and park maintenance suffered further. This process accelerated during the 1980s, a decade that began with a severe recession. By the end of that decade, the facilities were beginning to look shopworn. Signage faded, the buildings began to deteriorate and historic programs in the park became increasingly rare.

Further adding to the downward fortunes of the park was the disastrous robbery that the museum suffered in the mid-1970s. A ring of thieves had been hitting many of the small museums in the state, which were vulnerable because they lacked sophisticated alarm systems. The Putnam park museum was especially vulnerable because it had accumulated a large, impressive collection of eighteenth-century weapons, including more than eighteen flintlock muskets and pistols, which were the delight of every schoolboy who visited the displays. Unfortunately, they were also the delight of antique collectors. With their loss, the educational value of the museum was badly tarnished.

PARK CLOSURE AND THE RISE OF FANS

The year 1991 was filled with irony for Putnam Memorial Park. In June of that year, Ricardo Elias of Boston University's Office of Public Archaeology presented a massive tome to the Department of Environmental Protection (DEP) containing the results of an archaeology reconnaissance of the park that had been conducted the year before. According to the report's introduction, this was to be the first phase of a master plan for the development of the park.

The report's goals were threefold. First, to compile, study and evaluate all of the available documentary and historical material relevant to the park during its winter encampment and the park periods. Second, to assess the archaeological potential of the park through documentary research, field survey and subsurface testing. And third, to compile a database of information about the park that could be used to organize a master plan of development and an assessment of the potential contribution of archaeology for future interpretation of the park.[134] From all this, it appeared that the state intended to begin a rehabilitation of the park and that it would now enter a new phase of its historically interpretative life.

The economy, however, determined otherwise. By the early 1990s, it was again suffering from one of its periodic downturns. The governor, Lowell Weicker, faced with diminished revenues and increased budget demands, began a series of measures to correct the financial imbalances by saddling the state with its first personal income tax. Then came the severe budget cuts. Nine Connecticut state parks that were perceived as not having the potential to bring money into the DEP coffers were slated for decommissioning. Among them was Putnam Memorial Park, which was padlocked and its staff reassigned elsewhere, beginning a seven-year period of moldering inaction and continued deterioration.

During this period, however, a minor miracle occurred that would ultimately change the fortunes of the park. The neighbors of the park, reacting to the eyesore of an overgrown park and its potentially adverse effect on home values, used their own lawn equipment to cut the lawns visible from the road. They became the nucleus of a group that was later incorporated as the Friends and Neighbors of Putnam Park (FANS). But even the members' efforts did not stop the deterioration of the park buildings and other facilities. The pavilion was especially affected. Having lost its clerestory years before, it had been boarded up and closed to the public even before the park's overall closure. Now the building began a more rapid decay as the walls began to pull apart and the chimney, a later addition to the building, began to pull away from the north wall. More seriously, the sills, which were subject to the ravages of water from the leaking roof, were rotting, and it appeared that the building was doomed to destruction by neglect.

The turnaround for the park came on May 22, 1997, when it was formally recommissioned. In a grand ceremony presided over by Governor John Rowland, a group of DEP dignitaries (including the commissioner, Sidney Holbrook), several future members of FANS and Rosemary Paine's third-grade class, the gates were reopened. Even before that wonderful event, however, some DEP personnel and delegates from the Friends of Connecticut State Parks came to Redding to see if there was enough local interest to form a volunteer support group for the park. There was, and the Friends and Neighbors of Putnam Park was established in August 1997, only three months after the park reopened.

Support was truly what they provided. For the first couple of years after its resurrection, there was little money budgeted for maintenance of the buildings and grounds, much less money for the necessary rehabilitation. Under these circumstances, the members of FANS again volunteered to do the heavy manual labor necessary to begin to get the grounds back into shape. They did the weed-wacking, raking, clearing brush and opening the trails so that the park was once again looking presentable. It was during the process of clearing the brush from the heavily overgrown northern end of the Company Street that the untouched chimney remains were rediscovered, and the suggestion was made by FANS stalwart Harry Gibson, one of the park's greatest supporters, that archaeology be done in that area. The next year, 1998, we began the current archaeology program.

The park survey that had been made in 1991, just before the park closed, had recommended that a visitors' center be built to promote historical education of the park's origins and introduce it to the general public. Shortly after the reopening, the DEP developed a plan to build a new, up-to-date visitors' center on top of the hill in the southwest corner of the park, where the Boy Scouts had traditionally camped. This was hotly resisted by both Redding and Bethel as being too lavish for a rural park, generating an inordinate amount of traffic for this residential section of the towns. The plans were scrapped, and the move toward a visitors' center was refocused on the 1893 pavilion.

Meanwhile, saving the pavilion was beyond the volunteer efforts of the FANS members, although it remained high on their agenda. Money was needed for an architectural survey of the building to get recommendations as to whether it could be saved or would have to be torn down and replaced with something more substantial, if less authentic, to the park's origins. To the surprise of all involved, the verdict came back that the building could and should be saved, and a program was quickly developed to render architectural first aid. The roof was repaired. The bowing sides were bolted and drawn together, and the sills were replaced. The chimney, which had not been on the original structure, according to some of the earliest photographs of the park, was removed.

In June 2003, a request was put to the state's bonding authority for an appropriation of $2.4 million to completely overhaul the pavilion, which had been built in an era when electricity had not yet arrived and indoor plumbing was a luxury. The money was approved, but action was not taken until a year or so later. At that time, the old pavilion was taken down board by board—each piece being numbered for reassembly. A new foundation was laid, with modern plumbing for visitor restrooms, and the framing of the superstructure was constructed, allowing for modern amenities such as electricity, heat and air conditioning. The clerestory was reconstructed and fitted out for a superintendent's office. The circular windows that had always been open were fitted with glass to allow the climate controls to function. In all of this, as much of the original structure as could be salvaged was saved and incorporated into the new building, including even some of the original shingle siding. Today's visitor can tell the new from the old by the dark and light color of the wood in the interior of the building.[135] The new visitors' center/pavilion was formally opened to great fanfare by Governor Jodi Rell and the usual dignitaries in October 2005.

With the physical needs of the park being seen to, FANS members turned to developing several educational programs, which are annual and ongoing. The most popular of these programs is School Days. For a week in May every year, groups of schoolchildren are bused into the park from all over the county to experience a series of interpretive presentations put on by reenactors and members of FANS. These presentations range from demonstrations of marching and musketry to casting of ammunition, medicine of the Revolution, open-hearth cooking and the presentation of fife and drum music, as well as a chance to view the archaeological exhibits and listen to brief explanations of how artifacts are recovered and interpreted.

The Summer Craftsmen program brings Revolutionary-era artisans to demonstrate their crafts on weekends in July and August, providing educational entertainment, as well as a chance to walk the park and contemplate its features. More grandiose is the Living History Weekend, which runs in the fall every other year. This draws Revolutionary reenactors, both Patriot and British, from all over the Northeast to the park, where they camp and practice everything from mundane camp activities to grand skirmishes between colorful British and Continental soldiers. Even though the park was not a site of any battle, the maneuvering of troops, often with cannons and occasionally horse troops, is a great crowd pleaser, but more importantly it allows the public to talk to and interact with men and women who are experts in the Revolutionary period and thus learn far more than they ever did in their school classrooms.

The fourth program, the Winter Walk, grew out of an ironic observation made shortly after the park was reopened. Although the park commemorates the Putnam winter encampment, it is always enjoyed in the summer and is closed during the winter, when the camps were originally occupied. About 2000, it was decided that the park should be reopened one day during the winter and a tour given to allow people a chance to experience the campgrounds as they would have been when the New Hampshire troops along with the Canadians marched into the valley on the first weekend in December. That first year, the tour was conducted the day after a six-inch snowfall. Two reenactors trudged through the snow in front of the tourists, and it took no imagination to see oneself over two hundred years in the past, marching behind the silent ghosts of Lieutenant Colonel Dearborn and Sergeant Major Hawkins.

APPENDIX I

The Other Half of the Park

The modern visitor to Putnam Memorial State Park quickly becomes aware that there is another side to the park, the recreational area on the east side of Route 58. This area was not part of the winter encampment. There have been claims of collapsed chimney remains on top of the hill in the northeast corner that have appeared in the various park guides over the years, but our survey of this area showed that the piles of rock were not old and were probably the result of nineteenth-century farmers clearing the land of rocks to make it more efficient for grazing cattle.

The lake that dominates this section of the park was originally a swamp into which flowed three streams draining the historic side of the park and another one running south along Route 58. The swamp is really the source of the Little River, which is a tributary of the Saugatuck River several miles to the south. It became a lake only in 1891 with the formation of the old clubhouse.

Isaac Bartram, a principal founder of the Putnam Memorial Camp, was very familiar with the entire region, having grown up here and having worked on the park since its inception. He enlisted several gentlemen of Danbury and Bethel, and they purchased about one hundred acres of land extending from the Old Sherman Turnpike (Route 58) eastward to the top of the hill. He then constructed the dam where Pocahontas Road crosses the outflow of the swamp, creating the lake. On a rise above the southwest corner of the lake, he had a large clubhouse erected at which the members of the club could enjoy a good dinner and retire to enjoy an equally good cigar. Just below this, he built a keeper's house for the club's custodian.

The old clubhouse built near the newly formed lake in 1891. It was the scene of many area social functions until it burned down in the early 1920s. This is presently the site of the park superintendent's house.

The club grew to about fifty members and flourished for almost a decade and a half. As the original members died or moved away from the area, however, the club found that it was more and more difficult to maintain the buildings and grounds. Shortly after the turn of the century, articles in local newspapers told of dances being held in the clubhouse, mostly for young people, and dinners were being enjoyed by people other than club members, all in hopes of generating enough money to allow the club to continue.

Shortly before 1910, the property was sold to the Rogers Peet Company of New York and, for several seasons, was used as a summer camp and retreat for its clerks and other employees. Gradually, however, the club property became abandoned, and in the early 1920s, the clubhouse burned down. In 1923, the state became interested in the property, seeing it as a recreational adjunct to the park, and later that year it was purchased, effectively doubling the total area of the park. Shortly after the acquisition, a new house was constructed on the foundation of the old clubhouse. This became the superintendent's house, replacing the bungalow to the north of the pavilion that had served that purpose since the turn of the century.

APPENDIX II

The Military Hospital at Danbury

Although not part of the Redding encampments, the Danbury military hospital was an important institution in that it tended to the camp's seriously and fatally ill soldiers. This is also where the twenty-seven men who died during the Putnam Park encampment were treated and probably where they were buried, so the hospital is a part of the history of the park even if only peripherally.

Until recently, there was a mystery associated with the hospital's formation. According to Danbury's nineteenth-century historian, James Montgomery Bailey, during the Danbury Raid in April 1777, "there was an army hospital in existence here. It was established the month before, and was not touched by the British."[136] The mystery centers on why the British did not damage or burn down the hospital building, especially when they marched right by it on their retreat out of town.

The solution comes from a careful study of the Danbury Land Records. During the raid, the town records were burned, so the current records only begin right after the destruction. Ironically, the first deed in the first volume of these new records, dated July 17, 1777, was a warrantee deed from Joseph Wildman to Philip Turner of Norwich for six and a half acres of land on the corner of what is today Park Avenue and Pleasant Street.[137] Turner was the Director Surgeon of Hospitals for the Eastern Division, and the parcel of land was meant for a military hospital. The British, then, did not damage the hospital because it did not exist until after the raid.

The reason for creating a hospital in Danbury was given by General Washington in a letter sent to William Shippen Jr. in September 1778, just before the Redding winter camps were set up. In it he noted that owing to the anticipated movement of British troops eastward from New York, the large military hospital in Bedford was exposed to British attack. He therefore requested that the patients and hospital supplies be moved farther inland to Danbury. This same thinking had applied the year before, just after the raid, when the commander realized that the temporary hospitals near the coast in Stamford and near White Plains were at the mercy of British attack. The answer was to move inland, and Danbury, being a large supply depot for the Continental army, was a logical location for a permanent hospital facility. While it was true that this location had just been subjected to a raid, the chance of that happening again were slim given the large number of casualties that the British troops had suffered. The troops stationed in Redding during the winter were also a deterrent.

A description of the hospital must be vague at best. According to Bailey, "The Hospital itself was a one story building with a large garret in its steep roof. The first floor was divided into four rooms; the garret was of one room. The building was torn down many years ago by its owner."[138] Bailey's sources are not given, but his description was probably part of the local oral history that was so prevalent at the end of the nineteenth century, supplemented by a description of the building that was torn down within his memory, which was presumed to be the hospital building.

One piece of contemporary evidence that gives a more accurate picture of the hospital is the map that was made of Danbury in 1781, when the French army under the Comte de Rochambeau marched through western Connecticut. This map was one of several campaign maps drawn by the French engineer Captain Louis-Alexandre Berthier, and based on his other maps, which can be checked by still existing local landmarks, they are distinguished by a high degree of accuracy. In the lower portion of the map is a cluster of four buildings clearly labeled "hopital." These buildings consist of two long structures to the north and south, with two smaller flanking buildings to the east and west, creating a central courtyard.[139] One of these buildings may still exist as a private residence. The owners are history teachers who have done extensive research on the house and claim that, although moved slightly, it is one of the larger buildings in the array of four.

Another piece of evidence gleaned from the National Archives tends to support the description contained on the Berthier map. One of the microfilmed records for the Revolution contains a return from the hospital at Danbury for the period of October 20 to November 9, 1778. In that report, 186 men were treated and sent back to camp, 162 remained in the hospital convalescing and another 35 were still being actively treated. For a period of twenty days, the health facility treated or was still treating 383 people, indicating that it must have been a large collection of buildings rather than the small, one-story structure described by Bailey.[140]

Two of the patients were treated for pregnancy. This may indicate the presence of women in the Redding camps or the possibility that the hospital treated civilians. Given Hawkins's explicit comment about their being "wives and concubines" in camp, and given that the commanding officers were reluctant to expend scarce resources on civilians, especially women, it is most likely that the women who were laying-in at the hospital were from the camps.[141]

Bailey claimed that the soldiers who died "were buried in a plot of ground on Pleasant Street near the corner of Park Avenue. This burial place was held sacred by Mr. Wildman [a later owner of the property], who would not have it plowed. Some years after it was rented, and the tenant, being either ignorant of its former use or extremely practical in his views, turned up with his plow many bones and some relics in metal." The fate of these bones and relics is unknown. The field behind the hospital building/residence is still clear, and it is hoped that in the near future a method of remote sensing, such as ground-penetrating radar, can be used to see if anything remains of the final resting places of the Putnam encampment's dead.

The relationship between the military hospitals and the officers who had men in them is a subject that has been minimally explored. In a lengthy order issued from Washington's headquarters at Middlebrook on April 1, 1779, was a section that specifically dictated the duties of officers toward their indisposed men. Besides the typically endless lists of men, arms and equipment that he should draw up and continuously submit to the paymaster or quartermaster, there were careful procedures to be followed in the event that the soldier died or, worse yet, deserted from his sickbed. One section of the orders carefully stipulated the officer's daily duty toward his sick and tends to demonstrate the compassion that Washington had toward the men of his army:

> *The Field Officers will reside as near the hospital they superintend as conveniency will permit & Visit them as often as possible, they will order the Commsd.* [commissioned] *Officers under them to Visit the sick of their respective Wards at least twice a day. They will examine critically whether the Sick are well taken care of & if in their opinion there be any faults or neglect in their management to report the same to the Director Genl. of the Hospitals or some of his Deputies & if a remedy is not applied in a reasonable time then to report the Same to the Commander in Chief.*[142]

The later history of the hospital was clouded by controversy. By 1781, Turner had been replaced by John Berrien as the head Director Surgeon of the Hospital. In a letter dated February 25, General Washington wrote to him from his headquarters, then in New Windsor, New York, that it had come to his attention that he had in his hands "a quantity of hospital stores purchased for public use which you refuse to deliver alleging that they were procured on private credit." He then went on to forcibly explain that whenever a public officer purchases for the public, it is taken for granted that it is done on public credit. Berrien was then admonished to immediately relinquish the disputed goods to the proper authorities.[143]

This admonition was not a light one. In a letter dated at the same time as the one to Berrien, Washington wrote to Lieutenant William Torrey, who was instructed to proceed to Danbury with a small force of soldiers. He was there to present Washington's letter and demand for the stores: "Should he refuse to deliver the public Hospital Stores in his possession, you are to take them by force...Should you be obliged to use military force to obtain these stores, which I hope will not be the case, you will proceed with prudence in the execution of your duty."[144]

Apparently, military force was not necessary, and the disputed stores were packed into wagons and transported to Fishkill. In fairness to Berrien, it should be mentioned that there is a letter from him to Washington explaining that there had been a "misapprehension." The stores were not withheld because they had been paid for with private credit, but rather a superior officer had so purchased some of the stores, and Berrien was under strict orders to not release them to anyone except to his superior or his representative.

The controversy does give us a date for the closing of the hospital. The movement of the Danbury supplies to Fishkill coincided with the movement of the army's health facilities westward as the war was entering its final phase in 1781. As to the hospital property, it was transferred by Philip Turner into a trust for the United States on June 6, 1778. It remained in government possession until four acres of it, with the buildings, were sold to Ezra Star in April 1784. So it passed into a sequence of private ownership, and the hospital passed into local folklore.[145]

APPENDIX III

The Prehistory of Putnam Park

In the process of excavating the eighteenth-century levels in the park, we discovered that the site had been attractive to more than a ragtag group of Revolutionary War soldiers. At a depth of two to three inches below the occupation floor of the huts, we began to find a light scattering of quartz flakes. Although the soldiers were known to sometimes knap the flints of their muskets to get a little more use out of them after they had begun to wear out, they had never been known to knap quartz. It is a mineral that does not reliably produce sparks when struck against steel. These flakes, therefore, must have come from a process of making stone tools. Their position beneath the hut floors argued strongly that they were the results of prehistoric tool production.

Excavations at the officer's quarters in 2001 yielded confirming data. Not only were flakes found, but several of the projectile points, probably spear points, were found as well. All but two of these were broken, strongly suggesting that this must have been a hunting camp where prehistoric man retired after a day of hunting to refurbish the projectile points by rechipping them. If they were too badly broken, they simply cut the damaged point off its shaft and discarded it before replacing it with a fresh, sharp stone point.

The recovery of these broken tools was important because they were diagnostic. That is, they were typically made by a group of hunters and gatherers who lived in this area between 4,000 and 4,500 years ago, a period known to local archaeologists as the Late Archaic. The hunters of the Late Archaic, therefore, were wandering the hills of Redding about the same time as the great pyramids of Egypt were being built.

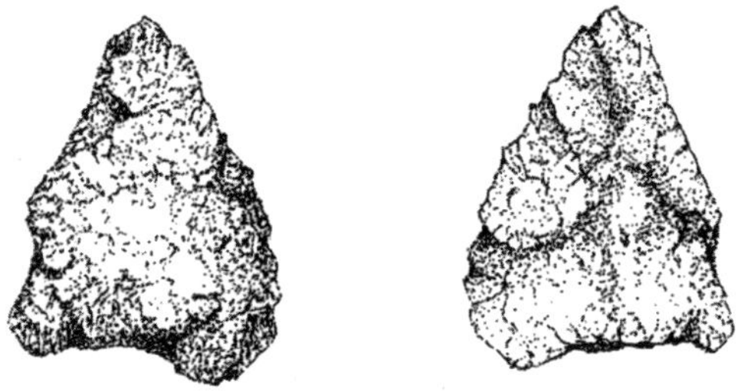

Small quartz projectile point of the Late Archaic variety. This is one of only two complete projectile points that are part of the evidence that attests to the prehistoric occupation of the site. *Drawing by Carol Franson-Serra.*

Their presence on the ridge top makes sense by just looking around. It is flat and located near a reliable source of water to the south. It is high, overlooking a wooded valley that, then as now, was likely traversed by deer runs, trails along which game animals could pass easily to new feeding locations. Those on the hill could watch approaching game just as Dearborn could watch over the troops for which he was responsible.

The site on the valley floor, where the enlisted men's huts were located, is a little more difficult to explain. It also is flat and in proximity to water, but it probably lay astride the game trails—possibly a location from which game could be ambushed, butchered and then eaten while the ever necessary process of refurbishing hunting tools was conducted.

Work on this aspect of the park's history has just begun.[146] Since the Revolutionary period was a research priority, the prehistoric component had been put off. This is now an area of ongoing research. Stay in touch with the park's website or, better yet, join FANS to receive the latest research on both the park's history and prehistory.

APPENDIX IV

The Legend of Philip's Cave

At the northern end of the park is a spectacular rock outcropping in the form of a steep, east-facing cliff. Down the front of this cliff, large boulders have fallen, creating natural rock fall caves. The largest of these has been the focus of a piece of folklore that exists in several versions and is still part of the park's interpretive signage, even though there does not appear to be any documentation for it.

According to the most common version, a soldier named Philip, who had lived in Putnam Park during the winter encampment, returned the next year—or, in some versions, several years later—and took up residence in the cave. His subsistence consisted of hunting, often in the farm yards of his neighbors. With the stocks of poultry diminishing steadily, the local farmers concluded that decisive action had to be taken, and one morning they tracked him to the cave and shot him dead. The threat to local livestock was eliminated, and the cave would forever bear the name of this martyr to free living.

In some versions, Philip is supposed to be King Philip, the Wampanoag chief who was the principal leader of King Philip's War. This version conveniently overlooks King Philip's death, which occurred in 1676, almost half a century before the formation of Redding and a full century before the Revolution. Other versions play equally fast and loose with historical reality.

The kernel of truth that so often forms the core of folklore such as this is, unfortunately, completely lacking. There is no documentation for Philip, who would be impossible to identify in the muster rolls, which contain a seemingly endless number of men with that first name. His death did not

The rustic walkway leading to Philip's Cave as it looked about 1900.

make the town's vital statistics, and a search of the local and state papers for mention of the crime has been fruitless. The lack of a dirt floor in the cave makes archaeology impossible. Even though it is quite possible that this shelter had once been used by an aboriginal hunter, any trace would have been picked up by relic hunters long ago, as would anything that Philip might have left behind.

In short, the story appears to be a complete fabrication, but the mystique surrounding this well-publicized hiding hole has delighted several generations of schoolchildren who have climbed into the cave that they think may have sheltered a murdered man.

Notes

Chapter 1

1. One of two journals that supply eyewitness accounts of the Putnam encampment was that of Sergeant Major John Hawkins, in McDonald, "Putnam's Folly." The short entries for the months of December to March 1778–79 will frequently be referred to and quoted without specific endnotes for each entry.
2. Henry Dearborn's journal contains the second eyewitness account of the events of the winter encampment, in Brown and Peckham, *Revolutionary War Journals of Henry Dearborn.* It, too, will be frequently referenced and quoted with minimal noting.
3. For statistics on the Quebec Raid, as for the other engagements mentioned in this work, I have relied on Boatner, *Encyclopedia of the American Revolution.*
4. It is well known that we were emerging from the climatic period known as the little Tudor Ice Age and that winters were colder during the Revolution than they are today. This is clearly reflected in the diaries and journals of the time. Joseph Plumb Martin, for example, who left the middle encampment on furlough during the early part of 1779, rode his horse to his uncle's house in Milford, Connecticut, across the mouth of the Housatonic River on the ice. This is a feat that has not been duplicated in living memory. Martin, *Private Yankee Doodle.*
5. Boatner, *Encyclopedia of the American Revolution*, 1,136.
6. Von Steuben, *Baron von Steuben's Revolutionary War Drill Manual*, 76ff.
7. McDevitt, *Connecticut Attacked*, 64.

8. National Archives, Revolutionary War muster rolls, reels M246, 43–48, and M246, 131.
9. Hall, *Life and Letters of Samuel Holden Parsons.*
10. John Read Papers, in the collections of the Connecticut Historical Society.

CHAPTER 2

11. Orderly book of Brigade Major David Smith, in the possession of the Connecticut Historical Society.
12. Poirier, "Camp Reading," 44.
13. Jennings, "Report of the Commission," 8.
14. Elias, "Winter Campaign of Starving."
15. For convenience, the hut pairs were numbered by Dr. Poirier from the southern end of the Company Street running northward and designated W or E depending on the row in which they lay. Working in the northern end of the street, our excavations were concerned with the huts E50, E51 and E52, as well as W51. Therefore, hut E51, the first we excavated, is the fifty-first pile of rocks in the east row. This system of designation covers just the enlisted men's huts.
16. Personal communication with park employee in September 1998.
17. Von Steuben, *Baron von Steuben's Revolutionary War Drill Manual*, 76 and plate no. 7.
18. Cruson, "Incidents of Regional Variation."
19. Elias, "Winter Campaign of Starving," 60.
20. *Newtown Bee*, September 4, 1896.
21. Revolutionary War muster rolls, M246, 42–48; Lesser, *Sinews of Independence*, 96ff.
22. Bailey, *History of Danbury, Conn.*, 100.
23. Cruson and Von Jena, "1999 Excavations at Putnam Park," 3.
24. Gibson, *Camp Reading.*
25. Elias, "Winter Campaign of Starving," 62.
26. Elias, "Winter Campaign of Starving," 66, quoted from the commissioners' reports of 1893 and 1903.
27. Washington's orders prohibiting entrenchment were issued in December 1778.
28. Todd, *Illustrated Guide to Putnam Memorial Camp*, 1890 ed., 25.
29. Todd, *History of Reading, Connecticut*, 34.
30. Grapeshot are iron balls about two inches in diameter that are placed in a canister that is used in a cannon. When fired, the canister breaks open, sending a cluster of this grapeshot into the enemy line like a gigantic shotgun.

31. Smith, orderly book, 8th Connecticut Regiment, 1st Brigade of Connecticut Infantry.
32. McDonald, "Putnam's Folly." The parentheses were added by Robert McDonald for clarification.
33. Cruson, "1998 Excavations at Putnam Park," 11.
34. Ibid., 9.
35. There will always be some movement of material vertically in the soil caused by frost and animal action. This is referred to as bioturbation, and it means that any individual artifact may be slightly above or below the actual floor line, but on average they will indicate when the floor level is reached.
36. Cruson, "1998 Excavations at Putnam Park," 11.
37. Schnadelback Braun Partnership, "Reconstruction of Soldier's Huts," 13ff.
38. Cruson and Von Jena, "2001 Excavations at Putnam Park," 6.
39. Schnadelback Braun Partnership, "Reconstruction of Soldier's Huts," 31.
40. Wilbur, *Revolutionary Soldier*, 66.
41. Von Steuben, *Baron von Steuben's Revolutionary War Drill Manual*, 76.
42. Schnadelback Braun Partnership, "Reconstruction of Soldier's Huts," 44.
43. Ibid., 22.
44. Wilbur, *Revolutionary Soldier*, 67.
45. For a statistical and detained description of this hut, see Cruson and Von Jena, "Different Lives of Officers and Enlisted Men," 6.
46. The analysis of the fireplace bone was done by Rose Drew, and the results are contained in a report in the possession of the author.
47. Todd, *History of Reading, Connecticut*, 147.

Chapter 3

48. Cunningham, *Uncertain Revolution*, 126.
49. Smith, orderly book for the 3rd Connecticut Regiment, 1st Brigade of Connecticut Infantry, orders for Camp Cleanup April 16, 1779.
50. Cruson, "1998 Excavations at Putnam Park," 6.
51. Cunningham, *Uncertain Revolution*, 100ff.
52. Pension deposition of James Sanford as a teamster from Redding, pension deposition dated October 22, 1833, National Archives.
53. Hall, *Life and Letters of Samuel Holden Parsons*, 205.
54. Smith, orderly book for the 3rd Connecticut Regiment, 1st Brigade of Connecticut Infantry, Adjutant's Orders on April 24, 1779, at Redding.
55. Poirier, "Camp Reading," 49.

56. Martin, *Private Yankee Doodle*, 151.
57. Hall, *Life and Letters of Samuel Holden Parsons*, 212.
58. Gibson, *Camp Reading*, 4.
59. Everest, *Moses Hazen and the Canadian Refugees*, 64.
60. Gibson, *Camp Reading*, 4.
61. The definitive work on American military buttons is Albert, *Record of American Uniform and Historical Buttons*. See especially page 7, where types of buttons are discussed.
62. Hanson and Hsu, *Casemates and Cannonballs*; Grim, *Archaeological Investigation of Fort Ligonier*.
63. Hanson and Hsu, *Casemates and Cannonballs*, 80.
64. Lindsay, *New England Gun*, 42.
65. Smith, orderly book for the 3rd Connecticut Regiment, 1st Brigade of Connecticut Infantry.
66. The difference in lifestyle between the officers and enlisted men of the Putnam winter encampment has been concisely summarized in Cruson and Von Jena, "Different Lives of Officers and Enlisted Men," 55–68.
67. See note 46, concerning the identification of these remains by Rose Drew.
68. Brown and Peckham, *Revolutionary War Journals of Henry Dearborn*, 154.
69. Jim Freebairn, personal communication, October 31, 1999.
70. The term "flanking" during this period meant defending (i.e., guarding against enemy attack).
71. General orders, May 19, 1779, in Smith, orderly book for the 3rd Connecticut Regiment, 1st Brigade of Connecticut Infantry.
72. These statistics were derived from Lesser, *Sinews of Independence*.

CHAPTER 4

73. Grumman, *Revolutionary Soldiers of Redding Connecticut*, 80.
74. The current fieldwork and research of Dr. Laurie Weinstein in the center encampment has led to new information on the presence of marginal peoples—African Americans in addition to Indians—that will eventually modify our view of the complexion of the camp population.
75. Brown and Peckham, *Revolutionary War Journals of Henry Dearborn*, 141.
76. Cruson, "Rural Parish in the Revolution," 132ff.
77. This version of Putnam's speech is taken from Grumman, *Revolutionary Soldiers of Redding Connecticut*, 81. It is substantially the same in its wording as in many other sources dealing with Putnam's life.
78. The order appears in an orderly book in the Henry Champion Papers of the Connecticut Historical Society.
79. Cunningham, *Uncertain Revolution*, 287.

80. Jones, orderly book kept for the 2nd Canadian Regiment, general orders of Colonel Moses Hazen of December 30, 1778.
81. Smith, orderly book, 8th Connecticut Regiment, 1st Brigade of Connecticut Infantry.
82. Orderly book kept by a member of Webb's Additional Continental Regiment.
83. Smith, orderly book, 8th Connecticut Regiment, 1st Brigade of Connecticut Infantry.
84. Martin, *Private Yankee Doodle*, 151.
85. Except for one, all of these courts-martial, including those of Edward Jones and John Smith, were taken from the orderly book kept by a member of Webb's Additional Continental Regiment. The Hazen court-martial was taken from Jones, orderly book kept for the 2nd Canadian Regiment.
86. All of the orders concerning the executions are taken from the orderly book kept by a member of Webb's Additional Continental Regiment.
87. The most scrupulous account of the executions is given by Grumman, *Revolutionary Soldiers of Redding Connecticut*, 82ff. Regrettably, he gives no sources for his information, so evaluating the finer details of his narrative is difficult.
88. Pension deposition of James Sanford.
89. Barber, *Connecticut Historical Collections*, 399.
90. Anonymous article in the *Newtown Bee*, October 23, 1891.
91. Humphreys, *Life and Heroic Times of Israel Putnam*, 164.
92. Dann, *Revolution Remembered*, 66.
93. The fact that there was a procession to Widow Sanford's house indicates that the actual lodge rooms were not in the house but rather at some other place a short distance away. The location of the lodge rooms is presently unknown. Plumb, *History of the American Union Lodge No. 1*, 35.
94. Ibid.

CHAPTER 5

95. Lesser, *Sinews of Independence*, 109.
96. For a full treatment of the road to Canada project and the politics surrounding the invasion of Canada, see Everest, *Moses Hazen and the Canadian Refugees*, 71ff.
97. Reeve, "Archaeological Assessment Survey."
98. A partial accounting of Hazen's stay can be found in John Read's account book in the possession of the Connecticut Historical Society.
99. All of the orders concerning the closing of the camps have been taken from Smith, orderly book for the 3rd Connecticut Regiment, 1st Brigade of Connecticut Infantry.

100. Such advertisements appeared in the *Connecticut Journal* during the month of April 1779.
101. Showman, *Papers of General Nathanael Greene*, vol. 3, 444.
102. Pension deposition of James Sanford.
103. Todd, *Illustrated Guide to Putnam Memorial Camp*, 27.
104. Lesser, *Sinews of Independence*, 112.
105. Olsen, "What Happened to the Huts?"
106. Ibid.
107. Ibid.; see also Cruson and Von Jena, "Soldiers Left…then What Happened."
108. Orderly book kept by a member of Webb's Additional Continental Regiment
109. Smith, orderly book, 8th Connecticut Regiment, 1st Brigade of Connecticut Infantry.
110. The number of inhabitants at its height considers a troop population of three thousand on paper. According to the muster rolls, this would have been about correct at the time they marched into town, although in later months, as troops were sent out on detached duty, the number would have dropped considerably.
111. Showman, *Papers of General Nathanael Greene*, vol. 4, 206.
112. See, for example, Martin, *Private Yankee Doodle*, 111ff.
113. Todd, *History of Reading, Connecticut*, 45.
114. Mayer, *Belonging to the Army*, 91.
115. The details of the Betsey Foote story are taken from her pension file, the original of which is in the National Archives. The story has been summarized in Cruson, *Mosaic of Newtown History*, 48ff.
116. Hoyt, *Benjamin Hoyt's Book*, pages are unnumbered.
117. Ibid.
118. Livermore, "A Journal," 335.
119. Orderly book of Poor's New Hampshire Brigade.

CHAPTER 6

120. Todd, *History of Reading, Connecticut*, 55ff.
121. Todd, *In Olde Connecticut.*
122. This attitude is most clearly stated in a plan for the layout of the park in Todd, *History of Reading, Connecticut*, 2nd ed., 46.
123. This account of the formation of the park came from an interview with Todd shortly before his death that appeared in the *Bridgeport Evening Standard*, August 21, 1927.
124. These two letters were discovered in a lot of unsorted governor's papers in the Connecticut State Archives.

125. An account of Todd's later years was included in a speech by Judge Samuel Saw of Redding on the occasion of the plaque's dedication, *Bridgeport Evening Standard*, March 3, 1931. Found in a scrapbook on Redding (section on Putnam Park) in the Bridgeport Public Library, Bishop Room.
126. Redding Land Records, vol. 25, 81.
127. This feature can be seen in some of the early postcards of the park. Archaeology has shown that it had no impact on the actual buried level of the Company Street.
128. Accounts of the park improvements in 1893 and after have been taken from the commissioners' minutes and from the periodic reports of the commissioners to the DEP.
129. *Newtown Bee*, September 4, 1896.
130. *Newtown Bee*, August 7, 1896.
131. *Newtown Bee*, July 9, 1897.
132. *Newtown Bee*, July 25, 1919.
133. A good account of the changing fortunes of the park during this period can be found in the newsletters of the FANS organization written by Harry Gibson. See especially the newsletter of May 2011.
134. Elias, "Winter Campaign of Starving," 5.
135. Gibson FANS newsletter, May 2011.

APPENDIX II

136. Bailey, *History of Danbury, Conn.*, 100.
137. Danbury Land Records, vol. 1, 1.
138. Bailey, *History of Danbury, Conn.*, 100.
139. Rice and Brown, *American Campaigns of Rochambeau's Army*, map 148.
140. Service records for Department of Quartermaster General and Commissary General of Military Stores, National Archives, microfilm roll M880, rolls no. 1 and 2.
141. Washington's attitude against the presence of women traveling with the army and partaking of army resources has been well and thoroughly researched. See Rees, "Number of Rations Issued," 14. Rees references Washington's many letters on the subject.
142. Smith, orderly book for the 3rd Connecticut Regiment, 1st Brigade of Connecticut Infantry, entry for April 1, 1779.
143. Letter from Washington to John Berrien, and another letter from Washington to William Torrey, both dated February 25, 1781. See website for the Library of Congress, American Memory, http://memory.loc.gov/ammem/gwhtml/gwhome.html.

144. Ibid.
145. These transactions are recorded in the Danbury Land Records, vol. 1, page 3, and vol. 3, page 71.

APPENDIX III

146. For a good preliminary analysis of the park's prehistoric artifacts that we excavated, see Von Jena, "Archaeological Site Report Putnam Park Officer's Hut: An Investigation of the Prehistoric Component," in Cruson and Von Jena, "Different Lives of Officers and Enlisted Men," 10.

Bibliography

Albert, Alphaeus H. *Record of American Uniform and Historical Buttons.* Fairfax, VA: SCS Publications, 1977.

Bailey, James Montgomery. *History of Danbury, Conn.: 1684–1896.* New York: Burr Printing House, 1896.

Barber, John Warner. *Connecticut Historical Collections.* New Haven, CT: B.L. Hamlen, 1836.

Boatner, Mark M., III. *Encyclopedia of the American Revolution.* New York: David McKay Co., 1966.

Brown, Lloyd A., and Howard, H. Peckham, eds. *Revolutionary War Journals of Henry Dearborn 1775–1783.* Freeport, NY: Books for Libraries Press, 1969.

Cruson, Daniel. "Incidents of Regional Variation in Winter Encampment Hut Construction: Huts and History at Redding Connecticut." Paper delivered at CNEHA annual meeting in Buffalo, New York, October 27, 2007.

———. *A Mosaic of Newtown History.* Newtown, CT: Newtown Tercentennial Commission, 2005.

———. "The 1998 Excavations at Putnam Park," 1999. Report on file with the Connecticut Historical Commission.

———. "A Rural Parish in the Revolution: North Fairfield (Easton)," 1977. Manuscript prepared for the Historical Society of Easton, in its possession.

———. "The 2002–2003 Excavations at Putnam Park," 2004. Report on file with the Commission on Culture and Tourism and Office of State Archaeologist.

Cruson, Daniel, and Kathleen von Jena. "The Different Lives of Officers and Enlisted Men at the Reading Winter Encampment of 1778–79." *Bulletin of the Archaeological Society of Connecticut*, no. 64 (2002): 55–68.

———. "The 1999 Excavations at Putnam Park," 2000. Report on file with the Connecticut Historical Commission.

———. "The Soldiers Left…then What Happened: The Archaeology of Deconstruction in the Redding Winter Encampment of 1778–79." Paper delivered at the Society for Historical Archaeology, Providence, Rhode Island, January 13, 2003.

———. "The 2000 Excavations at Putnam Park," 2001. Report on file with the Connecticut Historical Commission.

———. "The 2001 Excavations at Putnam Park," 2002. Report on file with the Connecticut Historical Commission.

Cunningham, John T. *The Uncertain Revolution: Washington and the Continental Army at Morristown*. West Creek, NJ: Cormorant Publishing, 2007.

Dann, John C. *The Revolution Remembered: Eyewitness Accounts of the War for Independence.* Chicago, IL: University of Chicago Press, 1980.

Elias, Ricardo. "The Winter Campaign of Starving: Archaeological Investigations at Putnam Memorial State Park in Redding and Bethel Connecticut." Office of Public Archaeology, Boston University, 1991.

Everest, Allan Seymour. *Moses Hazen and the Canadian Refugees in the American Revolution.* Syracuse, NY: Syracuse University Press, 1976.

Gibson, Harry W. *Camp Reading: Connecticut's Valley Forge 1778–79.* Redding, CT: privately published manuscript on file at Putnam Memorial State Park, 1998.

Grim, Jacob L. *Archaeological Investigations of Fort Ligonier, 1960–1965.* Annals of the Carnegie Museum, vol. 42. Pittsburgh, Pennsylvania, 1970.

Grumman, William Edgar. *The Revolutionary Soldiers of Redding Connecticut.* Hartford, CT: Case, Lockwood & Brainard Company, 1904.

Hall, Charles S. *The Life and Letters of Samuel Holden Parsons.* Binghamton, NY: Otseningo Publishing Company, 1903.

Hanson, Lee, and Dick Ping Hsu. *Casemates and Cannonballs: The Archaeological Investigations at Fort Stanwix, Rome, New York.* Washington, D.C.: National Park Service, 1975. Publications in Archaeology no. 14.

Hayes, John T. *Connecticut's Revolutionary Cavalry: Sheldon's Horse.* Chester, CT: Pequot Press, 1975.

Hoyt, Benjamin. *Benjamin Hoyt's Book.* Danbury, CT: Danbury Scott-Fanton Museum and Historical Society, 1977.

Humphreys, David, Colonel. *The Life and Heroic Times of Israel Putnam.* Hartford, CT: Silas Andrus and Son, 1853.

Jennings, John H. "Report of the Commission of the Putnam Memorial Camp Ground." Originally printed in 1893 but reprinted as an appendix of the 1903 report, Putnam Memorial Camp Ground.

Jones, John. Orderly book kept for the 2nd Canadian Regiment of Poor's Brigade, kept between September 23, 1778, and August 1779. Original in the possession of the Historical Society of Pennsylvania, Philadelphia, Pennsylvania.

Lavin, Lucianne. "Connecticut Prehistory: A Synthesis of Current Archaeological Investigations." *Connecticut Archaeology Today*, no. 47 (1984). Archaeological Society of Connecticut Bulletin.

Lesser, Charles H. *The Sinews of Independence: Monthly Strength Reports of the Continental Army*. Chicago, IL: University of Chicago Press, 1976.

Lindsay, Merrill. *The New England Gun: The First Two Hundred Years.* New Haven, CT: New Haven Colony Historical Society, 1975.

Livermore, Daniel, Major. "A Journal." *Collections of the New Hampshire Historical Society*. Vol. 6. Concord, NH: Asa McFarland, 1850.

Lossing, Benson J. *The Pictorial Field-Book of the Revolution.* Rutland, VT: Charles Tuttle Company, 1972.

Martin, Joseph Plumb. *Private Yankee Doodle: Being a Narrative of Some of the Adventures, Dangers, and Sufferings of a Revolutionary Soldier.* Boston, MA: Little, Brown and Company, 1962.

Mayer, Holly. *Belonging to the Army: Camp Followers and Community during the American Revolution.* Columbia: University of South Carolina Press, 1999.

McDevitt, Robert. *Connecticut Attacked: A British Viewpoint, Tryon's Raid on Danbury*. Chester, CT: Pequot Press, n.d.

McDonald, Robert. "Putnam's Folly, Putnam's Valley, Devil's Den. An Excerpt From the Continental Diary of Sergeant-Major John Hawkins, 'Congress' Own' Regiment, Relating to the Redding, Connecticut Winter Cantonment, December 1778–March 1779." In the possession of the Pennsylvania Historical Society, private transcription, 1998.

Noël Hume, Ivor. *A Guide to Artifacts of Colonial America.* New York: Alfred A. Knopf, 1969.

Olsen, Eric. "What Happened to the Huts?" *Clio's Current*, no. 15 (February 1992). Morristown, New Jersey, Morristown NHP.

Orderly Book for Poor's Brigade 2nd Canadian, September 23, 1778–August 5, 1779. AM.633. In the possession of the Historical Society of Pennsylvania, Philadelphia, Pennsylvania.

Orderly book kept by a member of Webb's Additional Continental Regiment, March 27, 1779–July 2, 1779. Original with the New Haven Colony Historical Society/New Haven Museum, New Haven, Connecticut.

Orderly book of Poor's New Hampshire Brigade during the winter of 1779–80, November 30–December 23, 1779. Original in the possession of the New Hampshire Historical Society, Concord, New Hampshire.

Plumb, Charles S. *The History of the American Union Lodge No. 1. Free and Accepted Masons, 1776–1933*. Marietta, OH: American Union Lodge No. 1, 1934.

Poirier, David A. "Camp Reading: Logistics of a Revolutionary War Winter Encampment." *Northeast Historical Archaeology* 5, nos. 1–2 (1976): 40–52.

Rees, John U. "The Number of Rations Issued to the Women in Camp." *Brigade Dispatch* 28, no. 1 (Spring 1998): 2–10.

———. "The Number of Rations Issued to the Women in Camp." *Brigade Dispatch* 28, no. 2 (Summer 1998): 2–13.

Reeve, Stuart A. "Archaeological Assessment Survey of Lonetown Manor, Redding, Connecticut," 1997. Report on file with the Redding Planning Commission.

Report of the Commissioners of the Israel Putnam Memorial Camp Ground to His Excellency the Governor of Connecticut. State of Connecticut Public Document, no. 43, 1903. On file at the Putnam Memorial State Park.

Rice, Howard C., Jr., and Anne S.K. Brown, eds. *The American Campaigns of Rochambeau's Army, 1780, 1781, 1782, 1783.* 2 vols. Princeton, NJ: Princeton University Press/Brown University, 1972.

Ritchie, William. "A Typology and Nomenclature for New York Projectile Points." *New York Museum and Science Bulletin* 384 (1971).

Schnadelback Braun Partnership. "Reconstruction of Soldier's Huts: Valley Forge State Park, Pa." GSA Job No. 995-5, Research Documentation, n.d. The report is on file at both Valley Forge and Morristown.

Showman, Richard. *The Papers of General Nathanael Greene.* Vol. 4. Chapel Hill: University of North Carolina Press, 1986.

———. *The Papers of General Nathanael Greene.* Vol. 3. Chapel Hill: University of North Carolina Press, 1984.

Smith, David. Orderly book, 8th Connecticut Regiment, 1st Brigade of Connecticut Infantry, 1779. Original in the possession of the Connecticut Historical Society.

Smith, Joel. Orderly book, 3rd Connecticut Regiment, 1st Brigade of Connecticut Infantry, 1779. Original in the possession of the Connecticut Historical Society.

Todd, Charles Burr. *The History of Redding, Connecticut: From Its Earliest Settlement to the Present Time.* New York: John A. Gray Press and Steam Typesetting Office, 1880. 2nd ed., 1906, Grafton Press.

———. *Illustrated Guide to Putnam Memorial Camp, Redding, Connecticut.* Connecticut: State of Connecticut, 1927.

———. *In Olde Connecticut, Being a Record of Quaint, Curious and Romantic Happenings There in Colonial Times and Late.* New York: Grafton Press, 1906.

Von Steuben, Frederick William, Baron. *Baron von Steuben's Revolutionary War Drill Manual.* A facsimile reprint of the 1794 edition. New York: Dover Publications, 1985.

Wilbur, C. Keith. *The Revolutionary Soldier, 1775–1783.* Philadelphia, PA: Chelsea House Publishers, 1997.

Index

W

About the Author

Mr. Cruson is a retired high school teacher who designed and taught courses in anthropology and local history. His abiding interest in these fields has led him to do extensive research and writing on the history of the towns of central Fairfield County, including Easton, Redding and Newtown, as well as conducting several archaeological investigations in these towns in an attempt to learn more about the lifestyles of their past citizens, both historic and prehistoric. His attempts to acquire more information about the early history and culture of this area has also led him to investigate deeply the subjects of rural slavery, vintage photography, early Connecticut architecture, colonial and post-colonial road building and early cemeteries and their grave markers.

Mr. Cruson is active in a number of organizations dedicated to the research and preservation of local history. He has been a member of the historical society in Newtown, where he lives, for forty years, having served as its president for five years in the early 1990s. He was also a charter member of the Easton Historical Society and served a number of years on its board of trustees and as vice-president. In addition, Mr. Cruson is active with the Heritage Preservation Trust of Newtown, Society of American Archeology and the Archaeological Society of Connecticut, for which he is currently serving as president. He is also the town historian for Newtown and served as the chairman of the Newtown Tercentennial Commission in 2005.

In a continuing attempt to disseminate information on the early history and culture of central Fairfield County, Mr. Cruson has lectured and conducted adult seminars in addition to conducting his courses in local history for the high school students of Easton and Redding. He has published several books, including *The Prehistory of Fairfield County*, *Newtown's Slaves: A Case Study in Early Connecticut Rural Black History*, as well as *Newtown* and *Redding and Easton* in the Images of America series. He has also published *Newtown: 1900–1960* in the same Images of America series. Most recently he has published *A Mosaic of Newtown History*, a collection of his essays, and the history of the Newtown Savings Bank, as part of the commemoration of that institution's 150th anniversary. He recently published *The Slaves of Central Fairfield County* (The History Press), and his latest book, *Stratford West Woods and Everett Road: The History of an Easton Community*, has just appeared in print.